CFO Guide to Doing Business in China

CFO Guide to Doing Business in China

CHING MIA KUANG

John Wiley & Sons (Asia) Pte. Ltd.

This publication is designed to provide accurate and authoritative information in regard to the
subject matter covered. It is sold with the understanding that the Publisher is not engaged in
rendering professional services. If professional advice or other expert assistance is required, the
services of a competent professional person should be sought.

Other Wiley Editorial Offices
John Wiley & Sons, Inc., 111 River Street, Hoboken, NJ 07030, USA
John Wiley & Sons, Ltd., The Atrium, Southern Gate, Chichester, West Sussex PO19 8SQ, UK
John Wiley & Sons (Canada), Ltd., 5353 Dundas Street West, Suite 400, Toronto, Ontario
    M9B 6H8, Canada
John Wiley & Sons Australia Ltd., 42 McDougall Street, Milton, Queensland 4064, Australia
Wiley-VCH, Boschstrasse 12, D-69469 Weinheim, Germany

Library of Congress Cataloging-in-Publication Data
ISBN: 978-0470-82373-6

Typeset in 11/13 point, Janson Text Roman by Thomson Digital

Printed in Singapore by Saik Wah Press Pte. Ltd.
10 9 8 7 6 5 4 3 2

Contents

Acknowledgments

The objective of this book is to share the practical experiences of doing business in China through various case studies. While there are many people involved whom I cannot name all, I am deeply appreciative to them for inspiring me.

I wish to thank the partners in my firm, Irene Yap, Jane Shi, Lynn Fan, Ryan Li, Yu DX, Tinna Cao, Echo Li, Lanny Liang, Wu Di, Brenda Li, Nancy Shen and many others who have helped me in preparing this book.

I also wish to thank Janis Soo, CJ Hwu, Louise Koh, Cynthia Mak of John Wiley & Sons, who have helped me greatly.

Lastly, I would like to thank my wife and my family members for their support.

Introduction

The Opening of the Chinese Market

The opening of the Chinese economy to the world has been going on for almost 30 years. It has transformed not just China itself but also many other countries and peoples all around the world. China's admission to the World Trade Organization in December 2001 witnessed a surge in the number of foreign investments in the Chinese market. In addition, the 2008 Olympics were held in Beijing, and the 2010 World Exposition will be hosted by Shanghai. The momentum for further foreign investments and domestic economic growth will only be greater and faster.

China's Peaceful Rise (和平崛起)

At present, the whole world is witnessing the peaceful rise of "The Dragon-China." China's ballooning trade surplus with the United States has reached US$ 204.1 billion. The huge foreign exchange reserves of US$ 1.3 trillion[1] have also allowed China to start exporting capital, and not just products, to the rest of the world. This has resulted in the recent establishment of the State Investment Corporation

(SIC),[2] which is responsible for managing US$ 200 billion of China's foreign reserves for key strategic investments abroad. One of the first such investments was the US$ 3 billion investment for a 10 percent equity stake in the leading U.S. private equity lynch pin, the Blackstone Group. The SIC has also promised to hold its investments in Blackstone for at least four years. More recently, the China Development Bank[3] pledged to support Barclays Bank's (UK) record-breaking bid to acquire Dutch bank, ABN AMRO,[4] which is being carried out together with Temasek Holdings, the Singapore government's investment arm. While we do not know whether these mammoth investments will bear fruit in the future, at least for now, China is willing to export capital as part of its peaceful rise to prominence. The allure of engaging China is constant. The government of Singapore is currently in a race against time, in the hope of concluding a free trade agreement with China in 2008.

Business people who go in and out of China, or simply do business with China from their home countries, inevitably exchange their views and experiences of conducting trade and businesses in China. In the last few years, China's laws, economic system, rules, and regulations have all improved tremendously. The search for knowledge, experience, and guidance on doing business in China has become more focused. Business people want clear answers that they can rely upon, rather than vague advice. They will not settle for hearsay. Foreigners who trade with Chinese parties, or invest in China are getting smarter. Many are from countries where the Chinese language is not traditionally spoken, but they are learning and mastering it. They have witnessed China's development, and they have gained more experience. They know that there are rules and regulations to adhere to, however complex they may be to carry out.

Transition—China Is No Longer Based on Pure *Guanxi*

Major developments have occurred in the financial, taxation, and accounting aspects of Chinese business. These developments have picked up speed as China has become more integrated into the international system (与国际接轨) after being admitted to the WTO at the end of 2001. With tremendous speed, China has adopted and utilized international financial concepts and practices such as those of other OECD countries. This has posed tremendous challenges for Chinese accountants, public accounting practitioners, domestic as well as foreign controllers, and CFOs who have to ride with the wave of this transformation. Foreign business people cannot simply avoid China and remain ignorant. From a macro perspective, greater transparency and complexity in the regulatory system have been evolving as a result of the development of the Chinese economy. Gone are the days when pure *guanxi*[5] "关系" was the solution to most of the problems encountered while doing business in China. While one cannot ignore the importance of *guanxi* "关系", it is now necessary to get the procedures right.

What a CFO Needs to Know in China

In today's world, no matter where they are based, most organizations and companies are plugged into the Chinese market to some degree. As a CFO of such an organization, you have to plug in yourself. Whether or not you are based in China, or whether you operate remotely out of China, it is necessary for you to understand the Chinese way of doing business.

Amidst the flux of changes and developments, business people have constantly been aware that to make money in China, they need a good CFO who knows China.

One of the key attributes is to understand Mandarin. The Chinese language *Lianhe Zaobao* (the main Chinese language newspaper in Singapore) reported in July–August 2008 that some bilingual trained and experienced CFOs from Singapore can command yearly packages of US$ 1 million working for multinational corporations.

In addition to linguistic capabilities, a CFO must maintain a high level of integrity. He or she must also be very conversant with China's financial, tax, and accounting practices. In short, many organizations will hire CFOs who have real-life, practical experience in China.

What You Can Expect from This Book

The focus of this book is to share real-life, practical experiences and examples that we have worked on while consulting for clients. We hope to provide a guide to the CFO who manages finance, accounting, and tax for companies doing business in China. Many have written books on how to do business in China, providing hard facts and statistics. This book hopes not to simply provide the hard-and-fast rules of how to do business in China, but also to touch on the special duties of a CFO in China.

It will demonstrate and elaborate on the soft and hard skills, as well as the real-life financial and accounting techniques required of a CFO doing business in China. We start off by looking at how a CFO should help his or her company when the organization is getting started in China, in matters such as investment and incorporation of business entities. Next, we guide the reader into understanding aspects of feasibility studies, currency control regulations, accounting practices, taxation, and so forth. Here, we focus on Key Aspects. We also discuss other important aspects of emotional quotient (EQ) that a CFO should know, such as Chinese business culture and human resource management.

Throughout the presentation, we will highlight real-life situations and case studies as much as possible. This allows readers to find guidance in addressing their own situations.

This book does not attempt to be exhaustive. Nobody can claim to be an "expert in China" (中国通), simply because China is so vast and is undergoing rapid change. Behind this lies a 5000-year culture and history. The key of this book is to focus on critical aspects of doing business in China, and to relate them to you. Readers can then make use of these lessons when similar situations surface now or in the future. We hope you will find the book useful and meaningful.

Endnotes

1. On July 11, 2007, the People's Bank of China announced that US$ 1.3 trillion foreign exchange reserves have been accumulated as of June 2007, an increase of 41.6% compared with the corresponding period in 2006. This figure is included in the Report of China's International Balances in the First Half Year of 2007 presented by the State Administration of Foreign Exchange ("SAFE") on October 31, 2007. Related reports and statements can be found under "Statistics and Reports" on the website of SAFE, http://www.safe.gov.cn/model_safe_en/index.jsp.
2. The State Foreign Exchange Investment Corporation (SIC) is a state-owned corporation established in accordance with Chinese Company Law with a registered capital of US$ 200 billion. Its investments are mainly focused in overseas and structured financial products.

3. The China Development Bank is a policy bank established by the Chinese government and is operated directly by the State Council.
4. On July 23, 2007, the China Development Bank formally signed a Share Purchase
   Agreement and a Memorandum of Strategic Cooperation with Barclay's Bank (UK)
   to support the latter's acquisition of ABN AMRO Bank.
5. *Guanxi* refers to the "relationships" or "connections" that one possesses. If one
   possesses a certain *guanxi*, one can get things done easily.

1

Getting Started I: Market Entry Strategy and Study

The Involvement of the CFO

As part of the investment study team, the CFO should naturally be a key person in the initial market study.

Some organizations, however, leave a lot of the main market study and analysis to the sales and operations people; rarely is the CFO involved at the early stage. But when doing business in China, this is not advisable because market entry study by operations and marketing people cannot ensure that an investment will be successful. In the context of China, the CFO's knowledge and input must be involved with the tax structuring of an investment entity or vehicle; issues such as how to carry out sales and billing; how to collect revenues, and so forth have to be conducted early. We will highlight these issues in greater detail in Chapter 2, "Getting Started II: Establishing the Entity."

It is important to have your investment project team consist of *both* sales and finance people. They need to consult not only with market entry consultants, but also with financial consultants to ensure that the starting-up phase has considered various issues exhaustively.

Below, we highlight some issues, which we consider critical, with respect to market entry strategy. Although the intention of this book is not to dwell on how the CFO looks at market entry in detail, it is important that the CFO be equipped with certain marketing or market entry tips while assisting the organization in doing business in China.

What Do You Do Best? (做生不如做熟)

It is amazing that a fair number of business people, especially the SMEs (small and medium enterprises), still approach the China market without some common sense. By lack of common sense, we normally mean that certain businessman are willing to conduct businesses that they are quite unfamiliar with. While a few may manage to succeed, most will not. The reason for failure may be simply overexcitement at China's domestic market size, too fertile an imagination, and a lack of analysis or market studies.

Bean Counter

For many years, an Italian businessman had been in the business of sourcing "corporate gift items" from China for export to Italy. In his home country, he was successful in branding and selling these gift items to corporate clients. At some point, he decided to set up an Italian coffee restaurant business in Shanghai. The whole idea started because he had a close contact that was roasting coffee beans in Italy. He then looked at the Shanghai market. Obviously, the market was huge with a population base of almost 20 million people. There was definitely a good market and business for restaurants and coffee cafeterias. He opened up five cafes in two years but lost about RMB 3 million. He later sank even further by trying to forge a joint venture with an un-familiar Chinese party. The joint venture was another failure. The business had to be liquidated eventually.

Do Not Be Driven by Excitement

This case illustrates a common mistake by SME businessmen. Some-times, certain multinational corporations (MNCs), and not just SMEs, can make the same mistake. People are easily seduced and driven by the vastness of the land and its 1.3 billion consumers. They lose sight of why they went to China.

In the above case, running a cafe and restaurant business is completely different from corporate gifts sourcing. Without prior experience in running a cafe, it is hard to answer market entry questions of where and how to position, pricing and product, and so forth. Moreover, the questions of leasing premises, hiring staff, and so on are very different from what they are in the home country. Even people who are in this business will run into great difficulties when they try to manage the same businesses in China.

Market Opening

For the products and services you are selling, the first issue is whether the laws allow for "sales of such products and services" in China. Although China joined the World Trade Organization (WTO) in December 2001, and has opened up many sectors to foreign investors, there are still various sectors or portions of sectors that remain closed.

For example, the utilization of raw rubber for manufacturing into rubber products (for example, shoes) is allowed. However, the trading of raw rubber itself by foreign investors is not permitted.

There are various reasons for closing off certain sectors to foreign investment. The most commonly cited reasons are politics, national security, and cultural sensitivity.

MOFCOM Investment Guide for Foreign Investors

China's Ministry of Commerce (MOFCOM) publishes and updates the Investment Guide for Foreign Investors (外商投资指导目录). The Guide categorizes industry sectors:

- Encouraged
- Restricted
- Prohibited

The Guide provides the legal bases for foreign investors' participation in the China market. Activities that are not specifically mentioned in the Investment Guide are largely permitted. In the next chapter, "Getting Started II: Establishing the Entity," we will discuss how to use the Guide in greater detail.

Chinese Proxies

Many businessmen who are willing to take high risks like to use "local Chinese individuals" as proxies to invest in areas where foreign investors are prohibited or restricted. Most of these business sectors are open to local Chinese individuals or corporations, but not to foreigners. We have often heard comments like "I have known my Chinese friend for many years, so there is no problem (没问题)."

Even though we have heard of many businesses that were supposed to have "no problems," we probably have seen more problems and failures than successes.

Proxy Offer

For many years, an American architect and interior design firm had used a local proxy individual to set up an interior design firm. At that time, the industry was not opened to foreign investors. The operation of the local proxy firm had been managed by the "local owner." The American "real investor" financed the operations through regular injection of funds on a "cost-plus" basis. Although the cost of funding had been acceptable to the American investor, it was not known that the local proxy was still being "employed" by another state-owned company. He was still receiving social security contributions from his former company. In addition, taxes had been grossly underpaid. This had inevitably put the American investor at great risks. It was decided that the proxy company should be closed down when the industry was opened to foreign participation. Further sums were incurred to settle the local proxy's costs and taxes.

Market Study

Market-study and entry consultants who have practiced extensively in China should be very good at this. Nevertheless, CFOs must know some aspects of the market, especially in specific relation to their companies' products or services. Market study includes the following areas:

- General geography and demographics
- Specific size of the market
- Consumer behaviors and Chinese culture
- Distribution channels
- Competition and value-added propositions (in the China market)
- Short-term and long-term strategies

Geography and Demographics

It is surprising, but true, that even businessmen who have already had dealings in China often lack such general knowledge. It is important to read up and gain a general knowledge of the history, geography, and demographics of China, right down to the specific province, city, or county—as far as possible.

For example, it is generally understood that Beijing, as the capital of China, is also the center of politics. Hence, most rules and regulations are very strictly enforced there. Shanghai and the Yangtze Delta Region cities, such as Hangzhou and Suzhou, are largely populated with entrepreneurial SMEs. The Pearl River Delta cities of Shenzhen and Guangzhou are flushed with huge numbers of trading and distribution activities. The rules and regulations are not so strictly enforced in these latter places, however. Such general knowledge about geography and specific locations is important in relation to your market entry strategy.

Size of Market

If you decide to go into a particular province or city, you need to know quite specifically the size of the market. Some foreign investors and businesses like to use their home base as a starting point; this is understandable because they are very familiar with it. This is especially common for business people from Singapore, which has a very small market base by most comparative standards.

Hence, when extrapolation is necessary, the city or province being studied in China appears "very big." The simple fact that China has a population of 1.3 billion often misleads people about their specific market. Today, China has about 98 cities with a population of at least 4.5 million. Majority of the population, however, are still living in the rural areas. However, we expect 200 to 300 million people to move to cities over the next five to 10 years. These rapid changes may create uncertainty at first, but reasonable statistical checks of the relevant areas, however, should create an accurate picture of the relevant market.

Chinese Culture and Consumer Behavior

Due to the widely varying experiences of the various age groups in China, it is always a tremendous challenge for businesses to understand the culture and behaviors of Chinese consumers, especially consumers of varying ages and locations.

Tangibility

Many consumers in China like to purchase products and services that they can physically touch, feel, and see. It is quite natural that in the past 30 years or so, rising standard of living has spurred the sales of consumer electronics such as televisions, refrigerators, and air-conditioners. Consumers are eager to buy things that they can easily touch, see, and feel. Their effects are immediate.

Intangible things, however, can be very difficult to sell.

For example, a marketing consulting company was selling its "strategy" to a Chinese company. It made a PowerPoint presentation. The charge for consulting time and effort was US$ 10,000. The consultant would easily have made a sale in a Western country. However, his Chinese entrepreneur client actually found the PowerPoint presentation to be very expensive. As far as the client was concerned, all he had seen were a few slides.

Perception of Product

Many foreign businesses who have succeeded with their products outside of China, often believe that these products have great potential and sales in China.

One must realize, however, that the vast majority of the Chinese population may not have even heard of the products. Time is required to educate consumers and advertise the products. Success cannot be achieved overnight. The Chinese like to describe this as "the process" (过程).

At the same time, foreign business people must accept the fact that other products, which are less known in the outside world, may have developed strongly, with early head starts through years of market development in China. They can, in fact, do better than "renowned products of the outside world."

Some good examples are Rado Watches and Ports International. These brands are not as highly regarded outside China, but they are very costly and enjoy great prestige as "The Brands in China."

Distribution Channels

Foreign businesses are beginning to understand that wide distribution networks are very difficult to build in China.

This is true of consumer products or intermediate products. The distribution of the population and the vastness of land sometimes make market-building efforts appear insurmountable, or costly, time-consuming and tedious.

In this regard, it is important to develop partnerships and alliances with trustworthy Chinese businesses. They can bring wider networks and distribution reach for foreign products. Obviously, the Chinese businessman will expect win-win situations, if they are expected to utilize their distribution networks in cooperative ventures.

Competition

Over the last 30 years, as China pursues an open-door policy, local Chinese entrepreneurs have been cultivated and groomed. Bringing traditional excellence to certain products, these local entrepreneurs have been formidable competitors to foreign investors vying for the same market share.

For example, Evian natural spring water may be very well regarded in the outside world, but it has a formidable competitor in Wahaha (娃哈哈).

The worldwide industry for port machinery and equipment has recognized Zheng Hua Port Machinery Company (ZPMC) which produces the largest numbers of cranes in the world.

Many more examples can be found, in a wide variety of industries. We are also seeing Chinese manufactures improve very quickly in quality as well as volume. One deputy general manager of a Shenyang heavy equipment firm illustrates this. Many years ago, his factory was producing parts for an overseas manufacturer. The latter assembled the parts with value-added technology and sold back the assembled equipment to China. However, today, the Shenyang plant has mastered the technology to do the same as the overseas company (he called him "老外"). In his words, previously he "worked for the 老外; now the 老外 works for him." These products and many others are creating fierce competition with well known brands throughout the world.

Many people believe that China's local products are lacking in quality. However, it is natural that when markets first open up, the first issue at hand, as they say in China, is to fill the "people's stomachs" (温饱). For that reason, the first wave of manufactured products are extremely cheap and of poor quality. However, going forward, China and the Chinese people know that to win, they must combine better technology with low cost to market better quality products.

Short Term or Long Haul

When writing about getting started in China, it is always a challenge to convince businesses to look at the long term. Opening up its market has brought about tremendous changes and development in China in the last 30 years. To some, 30 years is a long period. Others would say, however, that this is only the beginning of a rising era ("盛世"). Generally, the successful businesses we have seen have mapped out longer-term China strategies. They envision their organizations riding the economic boom in China over generations. In fact, most would view China as providing the economic engine and power for the rest of the other Asian nations.

Our advice is to look at the opportunities (and not one opportunity alone) over the long term. Short-term ups and downs will occur. Organizations that prepare their people to handle, tackle, and ride the waves over the long term should see greater earnings on this voyage.

2

Getting Started II: Establishing the Entity

What Investors Can and Cannot Do

Prior to entering the Chinese market, it is very important for foreign investors to understand the types of barriers and restrictions that they may face. Like many developing nations, China sometimes seeks to shield industries that may be vulnerable to strong competition from foreign companies. This is true especially for industries where China is still experiencing early-stage development. In recent years, the Chinese government has also been moving to attract foreign companies that will bring not only cash capital, but also investments in the form of greater value-added to certain target industries such as high technology, environmental protection products, and so on.

Foreign entities that seek to enter China are governed by the Ministry of Foreign Commerce (MOFCOM). Foreign entities will have to refer to the MOFCOM's Guide for Foreign Investors (外商投资指导目录).[1] This Guide classifies different business scopes according to three main categories.

- Encouraged projects (鼓励类)
- Restricted projects (限制类)
- Prohibited projects (禁止类)

Opening Up

An increasing number of sectors have opened up over the years as the Chinese government follows through with their World Trade Organization (WTO) obligations, which began after China became a member of the WTO at the end of 2001. It has since opened up various sectors of its market to foreign investors. For example, trading business conducted by foreign investors could only be established in bonded or free trade zones prior to December 2004. But now, such foreign-owned trading companies can be set up in any location. In another example, foreign enterprises were not allowed to establish head hunting recruitment agencies before mid 2006. But now, foreigners are allowed to own such companies through joint ventures with a Chinese partner, and the foreign ownership is allowed up to 70 percent equity.[2]

Investment projects that do not fall under the first three categories are regarded as permitted projects. Various policies will apply to various categories of projects (Permitted Category). Generally, it is easier to set up a Foreign Invested Enterprise (FIE) within the Encouraged or Permitted projects category. The foreign invested enterprise could enjoy more preferential treatment from business and tax perspectives. However, with the latest corporate tax reform, effective January 1, 2008,[3] many of the preferential tax incentives have been abolished.

The Ministry of Commerce (MOFCOM) has overall responsibility for approving the formation of FIEs, and for issuing approval certificates. The local MOFCOM authorities undertake the examination and approval procedures. Under normal circumstances, the following main documents should be submitted to support these applications:

- Project Proposal
- Letter of Intent
- Feasibility Study Report
- Articles of Association
- Joint Venture Contract.

However, the list of documents required for submission may vary, depending on the location and the types of operation.

After obtaining the Approval Certificate from the MOFCOM, the FIE has one month to register with the local Administration for Industry and Commerce (AIC) in the relevant locations in order to obtain a Business License. A whole range of other licenses will need to be obtained; we will discuss these in detail in the latter part of this chapter.

Four Main Types of Entities

There are four main different types of business entities in China for foreign enterprises. These are

1. Wholly Foreign Owned Enterprise (WFOE)
2. Equity Joint Venture (EJV)
3. Co-operative Joint Venture (CJV)
4. Registered Office (RO)

The different types of entities are described in the following table on pages 12–14.

WFOE or RO?

There are distinct differences between these two types of foreign entities operating in China. The basis for choosing between the two rests fundamentally with the objectives of the foreign investor's business in China.

Why RO?

Many foreign investors' first foray into China is to set up a Registered Office (RO). The registered office is considered to be a direct extension of its parent company, and is normally used for doing market research for that parent company. It is not an independent legal entity, and its activities must not generate revenue directly for itself. Hence, it is generally regarded as a very safe bet for entering China without having to put too much at risk. Foreign investors getting into sectors that are newly opened will normally set up an RO.

	WFOE	EJV	CJV	RO
Pros	— Foreign investor has 100% equity control and management.[1]	— Chinese partner may provide land, building, equipment, as well as existing, customers. — Make use of Chinese partner's licenses, which are not open to WFOEs. — Profit and risk are shared in proportion to the equity of each partner.[2]	— Chinese partner may contribute land, building, equipment, as well as existing customers. — Make use of Chinese partner's licenses, which are not open to WFOEs. — Flexible arrangement in the form of cooperation, profit and responsibility sharing.[3]	— Quickest way to set up. — Lowest risk to allow initial market testing.
Cons	— Cannot set up WFOE in specific industries; as the market sector may be closed to foreign investors.	— Foreign partner can only own a certain amount of equity as allowed under the Guide. — Does not have full equity control and management.	— Same as EJV.	— Cannot engage in direct business activities or enter into contracts. — Must engage local agent to hire local staff.

Shareholdings	— Foreign investor(s) contribute 100% of registered capital.	— At least one foreign investor, and one Chinese investor. Foreign investor contributes at least 25% of registered capital.	— Same as EJV.	— Not applicable.
Governance	• One managing director, or a board of directors (BOD) of at least 3 directors.[4]	• BOD of at least 3 directors.[5]	• BOD, or joint management committee of at least 3 directors.[6]	• Chief representative represents the foreign investor company.
Tax	• Exposed to company income tax, VAT, business tax, individual income tax.[7] • Enjoy tax incentives such as "Two-year Free and Three-year Tax Reduction".[8] • WEF Jan. 1, 2008, most of the tax incentives have been abolished.[9]	• Same as WFOE.	• Same as WFOE.	• Taxation on expenses on a deemed income basis, mainly on company income tax, business tax, and individual income tax.

(Continued)

	WFOE	EJV	CJV	RO
Reporting and Compliance	• Monthly report, quarterly report, annual audit and annual inspection.[10]	• Same as WFOE.	• Same as WFOE.	• Monthly report, quarterly report, and annual audit.
Time for set-up	• 3–4 months.	• 3 months.	• Same as EJV.	• 2–3 months.

[1] See Article 2 of the Law of Wholly Foreign-Owned Enterprises.
[2] See Articles 1, 4, and 5 of the Law of Sino-Foreign Equity Joint Ventures.
[3] See Articles 1 and 2 of the Law of Sino-Foreign Contractual Joint Ventures.
[4] See Article 45 of China Company Law.
[5] See Articles 31 and 32 of the Implementation of the Law of Sino-Foreign Equity Joint Ventures.
[6] See Article 24 and 25 of the Implementation of Sino-Foreign Contractual Joint Ventures.
[7] See Articles 48–51 of the Law of Sino-Foreign Contractual Joint Ventures.
[8] See Article 8 of the Corporate Income Tax Law 2008.
[9] See the Corporate Income Tax Law 2008.
[10] See Article 14 of the Law of Sino-Foreign Contractual Joint Ventures and Chapter 9 of the Implementation of Law of Wholly Foreign-Owned Enterprises.

Why WFOE?

On the other hand, the Wholly Foreign-Owned Enterprise (WFOE) is a 100-percent wholly foreign-owned subsidiary doing business in China, and hence, is a totally independent legal entity. In essence, it is a "locally incorporated company" enjoying almost the same business rights as local companies, except that it is totally foreign controlled and funded. Foreign investors who want to conduct business and generate revenue directly will choose the WFOE. Enterprises that wish to conduct trading can, as of December 11, 2004, set up a type of WFOE, called the Foreign Invested Commercial Enterprise (FICE). The FICE allows the enterprise to directly conduct importing, exporting, and other auxiliary activities.[4] The business scope of a typical FICE includes importing, exporting, wholesaling, distribution, sourcing, commission agency (exclude auctions) for [PRODUCTS] and related [PRODUCTS][5], and provide relevant supporting services.

RO to WFOE?

Many foreign enterprises opt to set up an RO when they first enter the Chinese market, before converting to a WFOE when the industry that they want to enter opens up. Normally, they do this when they feel that enough groundwork has been done, and the business operation is ready to launch into sales and marketing.

RO to WFOE

An American architectural firm set up two ROs when the architectural market was still inaccessible to foreigners. One was set up in Shanghai, and the other in Beijing. In 2007, after gaining enough knowledge and experience in China's design and architectural market, the firm decided to set up its own WFOE when the government deregulated the sector. Take note that in most situations, it is not possible to convert an RO directly to a WFOE. The parent company must start off by setting up a separate WFOE and then, deregister the original ROs.

Why Not RO? Why WFOE?

Although it makes perfect sense for foreign enterprises to switch from an RO to a WFOE when the market opens up, there are always a few exceptions. Depending on the business strategies of the foreign enterprises, it may be more advantageous for them to maintain the status quo despite the opening of the market. Some ROs act as the liaison partners for their foreign parent company, when sourcing for suppliers and customers. The contacts made will be passed directly to the parent company, who will then conduct international trade directly. From the foreign enterprise's point of view, they are saving the hassle of setting up a WFOE to distribute. Ultimately, what matters the most is not just the legality issues that one must consider; the commercial viability and business model of the investor are equally important.

What About JVs?

Many sectors may not require a foreign investor to have a Chinese Joint Venture partner now that the Chinese market is opening up: for example, in the food and beverages business, franchise, and retailing. Previously,

---

Partnership Agreement

The head hunting and executive search business was not opened up until the second half of 2006. Now that the industry is opened-up, foreign investors can take a maximum 70 percent equity stake in a firm. A local partner must take the remaining 30 percent. The client was reluctant to run the firm as a joint partnership but at the same time, knew it had to adhere to the regulations. Hence, it found a Chinese partner who acted as a proxy. Even though the foreign investor had contributed the entire capital, 30 percent control was legally ceded to the local proxy.

Essentially, the head hunting and executive search industry requires practitioners to acquire an intermediary license. It is necessary to obtain the Human Resource Certification, and this can be done more easily through the Chinese partner, even though the entire capital may be provided by the foreign investor.

foreign investors could only access these sector by setting up a Co-operative Joint-Venture (CJV) with a Chinese partner. Now they need not involve a Chinese partner. However, many foreign enterprises still prefer to enter the China market through a Chinese partner. This way, the foreign investor can tap the resources of the Chinese partner, who in turn, can safeguard the foreign investor's position in an unknown foreign land.

General Set-up Procedures

Incorporation of a WFOE

Basically, there are three different phases in the incorporation process.

Name Application

Phase 1

i) Name application   This is to be done with the Local Administration and Industry of Commerce (AIC, 工商局). There is a standard format for one to choose a Chinese name for the business entity. The format is as follow.

> *First Word*—Company Name
> *Second Word*—Activity (for example, trading, 贸易)
> *Third Word*—Location of business operation (for example, Shanghai, 上海)
> *Fourth Word*—Company Legal Structure (for example, Limited Liability 法律责任公司)

The use of "China," "Sino," "International," and certain other words are not permitted in the Chinese name unless special approval is given. They are, however, permitted in the non-Chinese name.

Phase 2

After the completion of *Name Approval Notification*, the *Approval Letter* and *Approval Certificate* must be registered next.

The Articles of Association, Feasibility Study Report, and the Lease Agreement must be submitted to the local Foreign Economic and Trade Commission (外经委). After reviewing the documents, the local Foreign Economic and Trade Commission will issue the approval letter and certificate (批准证书) within 10 to 15 working days.

Articles of Association (章程)

Purpose: The *Articles of Association* and the *Constitution* of the company are important documents that describe the shareholders, capital, business scope, and so forth. They govern and regulate the running and management of the company. The *Articles of Association* have to be approved by the Foreign and Economic Trade Commission. They also have to be registered and filed with the Commission.

Feasibility Study Report (可行性研究报告)

In the approval process, the Foreign Economic and Trade Commission requires the foreign investor to provide an analysis of the economic feasibility of the investment. When submitting the feasibility report, the investor needs to include a simple analysis of future profit and loss, as well as forecasted returns on the investment.

Lease Contract (房屋租赁合同)

A lease contract for proper business premises is needed when applying for the *Approval Certificate*. The investor will be awarded this when he or she leases premises for the business.

- Within 30 days of obtaining the approval certificate, the foreign investor will need to apply for the *Business License* (营业执照) from the SAIC (工商局). After obtaining the *Business License*, the foreign entity is then able to operate in accordance with the business scope that is described in the *Articles of Association*.
- Some key applications and certificates must be applied for in the next process. These include
  - Organization Code Registration Certificate (组织机构代码证) from the Organization Code Registration Bureau (组织机构代码局)
  - Statistics Registration Certificate (统计证) from the Statistics Bureau (统计局)
  - Foreign Exchange Registration Certificate (外汇登记证) from the Foreign Exchange Bureau (外管局)
  - Tax Registration Certificate (税务登记证) from the Taxation Bureau (税务局)
  - Custom Registration Certificate (海关登记证)

Capital Verification

Phase 3

i) Capital Verification (验资)   Any fresh injection (增资) of *Capital/Registered capital* (注册资本) will have to undergo a capital verification procedure. This can only be done by a China Certified Public Accountant. The foreign capital will be maintained in a foreign capital account (usually in U.S. dollars), and later converted into Renminbi (RMB) in the RMB basic account for operational use.

The incorporation of an RO is much simpler than that of a WFOE. For easy reference, the following table outlines the differences between the two.

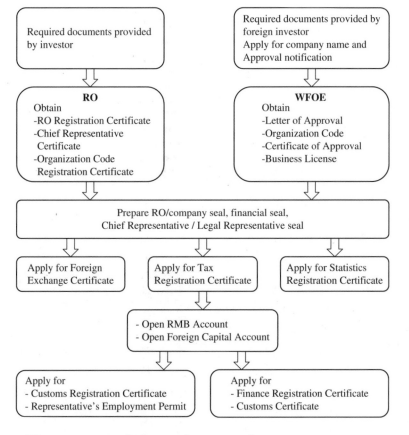

The process may take longer than expected

The chart simplifies the overall process of incorporation for easier understanding. In reality, the processes are more complex and tedious.

Each of the boxes depicted in the chart may contain several detailed processes involving form filling, translation, presentation of information, authorized signatures, and so forth. The incorporation process may take longer than the stipulated three to four months (for WFOE), or two to three months (for ROs). A lot of care and effort is needed to apply and obtain the multiple certificates, and stamps. Any glitches in one area may delay the later stages.

Registered Capital and Total Investments

For foreign invested enterprises, there are two important concepts to understand: Total Investment (TI) and Registered Capital (RC). Total investment refers to the amount, including the registered capital and funds raised by the company, that is required for the intended project of the Foreign Invested Enterprise (FIE). Registered capital is the total capital contribution that should be injected by the shareholders. It can be contributed by way of cash, physical assets, intellectual properties (IP), land use rights, and so forth. Normally, the cash contribution should not be less than 30 percent of the RC.[6]

   This sum of capital must be subject to a mandatory process called Capital Verification. This is to verify that the sum of capital has been

---

Taxing Issue

One foreign investor applied to inject US$ 1.2 million as Registered Capital, and US$ 700,000 was supposed to be in the form of Import Value Added Tax (VAT) exempted equipment. He was given approval on paper by the Ministry of Commerce to be exempted from Import VAT (VAT is 17 percent).[7] However, when the equipment was imported, the Customs Department did not allow the tax exemption. Apparently, the client did not explain the technological aspects of the equipment to the Customs Department clearly. It is the high technology status of the intended equipment (used as Registered Capital) that generally, allows a company to claim a VAT exemption. Finally, the client provided clearer explanations, and resubmitted documentation with proper descriptions, and the capital equipment was later imported with VAT exemption.

injected by the investor, and is genuinely used for the business. This is part of the Chinese government's continued efforts to weed out bogus investors who remove the capital after their incorporation, leaving a business entity with only a fictitious amount of registered capital.

Capital Verification Is Important

The Chinese government takes a very serious view in implementing Capital Verification, which must be done by a certified Chinese Certified Public Accounting firm.

Fast Forward

After a freight forwarding company was incorporated, it was required to fulfill the registered capital commitment. After consulting with a local business advisory firm, the investor was told that the registered capital that he pledged could be taken back. Hence, heeding the advisory firm's advice, he went on to withdraw his registered capital not long after injecting it, thinking that this was legal. The local authorities soon found out and decided to impose penalties. The freight forwarding firm's business license, which was a very good one that covered an extensive business scope, was suspended. Although it was not the freight forwarding firm's intention to mislead the authorities, not knowing the importance of complying with the capital verification regulations resulted in a huge price being paid.

Post-Incorporation

Challenges

The challenges of establishing an entity do not end with legal incorporation. In fact, there is still a huge amount of work needed to be done in the post-incorporation stages.

One of the key issues in the post-incorporation procedures is applying for the Value Added Tax Status (called the General Taxpayers

Status or Small-scale Taxpayers Status). This is true particularly for manufacturing and trading companies. Depending on their level of sales turnover, it is only after applying for such a status that the entity can start to issue tax invoices (for trading, distribution, and wholesale business) in their business operations.

Manpower Concerns

Complying with the local manpower legislation, and managing a proper payroll and human resource system are vital as well. Post-incorporation social security registration must be done for all staff and employees in the company. Complying with the social contribution can be complicated at times, and it is essential that a proper payroll and human resource system be in place.

Taxation

As described in Chapter 5, "Taxation," since China's taxation system is somewhat more complex than those of many other countries, it is especially important that a proper taxation and accounting system be adopted.

All the above, together with many other concerns in the post-incorporation stage, make the entire pre- and post-incorporation process long and arduous. Many companies, in fact, opt to outsource the entire incorporation and post-incorporation processes. Later chapters, including Chapter 5, "Taxation"; Chapter 6, "China's 2008 Corporate Tax Reform"; Chapter 8, "Hiring and Employment"; and Chapter 9 "The 2008 Labor Contract Law" will provide more detail on the issues that have been outlined in this chapter.

Endnotes

1. Catalogue for the Guidance of Foreign Investment Industries, October 31, 2007.
2. According to the Interim Administrative Regulations on Sino-Foreign Joint Human Resource Agencies issued jointly by Ministry of Personnel, Ministry of Commerce, and the Administration of Industry and Commerce of the People's Republic of China, which came into effect on November 1, 2003, and the *Decisions on Amendments of the Interim Administrative Regulations on Sino-Foreign Joint Human Resource Agencies*, issued by the same authorities, and the *Arrangement for Enhancing the Trade*

Relationship of Mainland, Hong Kong and Macau, the registered capital for such agencies must be at least US$ 300,000, among which the Chinese party shall contribute no less than 51 percent, and the foreign investor no less than 25 percent; for Hong Kong and Macau investors, foreign investors are allowed to own no more than 70 percent of the agency's equity, and the minimum registered capital is US$ 125,000.

3. See the new EIT Law, which came into effect on January 1, 2008.
4. See The Ministry of Commerce of the People's Republic of China [2004] No.8: Measures for the Administration on Foreign Investment in Commercial Fields.
5. The investor can fill in the names and products in the typical statements for the FICE's business scope.
6. See relevant provisions of the Law of Sino-Foreign Contractual Joint Ventures, the Law of Wholly Foreign-Owned Enterprises, and the Law of Sino-Foreign Equity Joint Ventures.
7. According to Article 2 of the Interim Regulations on Value Added Tax, the VAT rate is 17 percent. In the meantime, the Notice on the Supporting Taxation Policies for the Culture Industry in the Cultural System Reform (Caishui [2005]2) issued jointly by the Ministry of Finance, the Customs Administration, and the State Tax Bureau has stipulated situations of exemptions of import value added taxes.

3

China's Accounting System

M any foreign investors and CFOs are trained in Western accounting systems. To manage the accounting functions of business
operations in China, however, requires a good understanding of the
accounting system in China.

The Stages of Evolution of China's Accounting System

In the last 30 years of economic reform, the Chinese accounting system
has gone through several developments. After many years of consistent
change, the improvement of the system continues to be an ongoing
process. We can classify the development of the accounting regulatory
system into four different stages.

The first stage started in 1993. The direction was set by the China
National People's Congress when it passed the Accounting Law of the
People's Republic of China. This initial accounting legislation was, in
fact, first announced in 1985, and went through its first amendment in
1993. In 1999, it went through its second amendment; the changes
took effect on July 1, 2000.

The second stage took place when very significant legislation was
announced by the government on June 21, 2000, which focused on the
Regulations on Corporate Financial Accounting Reports. It took effect
on January 1, 2001. The purpose of all this legislation was to perfect
the accounting systems.

The third stage of the accounting development came when recommendations were made by the Minister of Finance. These recommendations focused mainly on the accuracy of accounting practices, and the ethics of proper accounting practices. In 2002, the ministry promulgated 16 enterprise accounting accuracy recommendations, proper enterprise accounting ethics, financial enterprise accounting ethics, and several recommendations for special industries. Effective January 1, 2005, a new legislation was passed to improve the accounting practices of small enterprises. Such enterprises may follow normal accounting practices for Small Enterprises. Alternatively, they can also choose to comply with the Enterprise Accounting Practices. Taking China's economic growth requirements into consideration, and in an effort to improve China's accounting accuracy standards, as well as to align it with the rest of the world, on February 15, 2006, the Ministry of Finance announced a total of 22 new recommendations on accounting practices. These were in addition to the original 16 accounting recommendations.

The fourth stage of the accounting practice development started in 1986. The legislation included the Measures on Accounting Archives that were first announced by the Ministry of Finance on June 1, 1986, and amended on August 21, 1998 (implemented on January 1, 1999). This legislation also covered Accounting Management Methods, Basic Accounting Work Regulations, and Internal Accounting Controls Regulations.

The Chinese accounting system has developed at the same pace as the general economic reform. This is a natural progression because the Chinese government realizes that accounting and financial systems must be able to support businesses that invest in China.

Foreign accountants in China sometimes complain about the old-fashioned ways of the Chinese accounting system. In fact, this shows a lack of understanding of the developments that have taken place over the years. This lack of awareness, in many instances, has caused accountants or business people to encounter problems while doing business in China.

New Enterprise Accounting Standards

The New Enterprise Accounting Standards were implemented on January 1, 2007, on all China listed companies, and all other enterprises are encouraged to follow suit.[1] This measure is one of the most important steps in China's accounting history.

The New Enterprise Accounting legislation adopts the direction of one basic piece of legislation, with 38 other pieces of comprehensive legislation as guides. The basic legislation forms the framework of the entire system, the main accounting regulatory objectives, requirements for accounting practices, accounting principles, and other important accounting requirements.

The accounting standards can be divided into three different categories:

- Ordinary standards
- Special work standards
- Reporting standards

The new Chinese Generally Accepted Accounting Practices (GAAP) are moving toward greater harmony with International Financial Reporting Standards (IFRS). They are also a demonstration of the bold steps taken by the Chinese government and accounting industry to support the next phase of deepening economic reforms.

Nevertheless, there are still differences from International Financial Reporting Standards (IFRS) in certain aspects of Chinese accounting practices. So, how does a foreign company with a subsidiary in China reconcile the local accounting books for consolidation when a different set of accounting policies are required to be adopted in China?

Reconciliation of Books Between Chinese and International Standards

In practice, the China accountant (of a foreign parent company) must understand the parent company's accounting policies and procedures. While the local Chinese GAAP have to be adopted, the financial statement entries will be adjusted towards the parent company's policies, be it U.S. GAAP or International Financial Reporting Standards for consolidation purposes. The CFO must thoroughly understand the adjustments that must be made to the books of the Chinese subsidiary when they are consolidated with the parent. The CFO must also understand the impact of these adjustments.

Depreciating Assets

A good example of this occurred in a case when port equipment was depreciated over 15 years in the company accounts of a local Chinese joint venture, while the policy of the foreign joint venture was to depreciate over five years partially. This resulted in higher profits for the joint venture company in the earlier years. Given that it was depreciated over tax exemption years, this was beneficial from both profit and cash repatriation perspectives. The joint venture foreign party needed to adjust the depreciation figures when the accounts were consolidated.

Accounting Personnel and Organizational Structure

An enterprise must establish the necessary accounting systems. Companies should engage the services of qualified accountants. Those who have neither an adequate accounting system nor qualified accountants should engage the professional services of accounting firms, or equivalent parties that are able to carry out the accounting functions on behalf of the firm. The accounting firm should possess a certificate of qualification from the Chinese government. The cashier and the other accounting functions, such as recording, should not be undertaken by the same person. Segregation of duties is a very important form of checks and balances in the Chinese accounting system.

Different Views of the Accounting Profession in China and in the West

Traditionally, the Chinese have accorded greater social status to accountants. For example, Chief Financial Officers in some Chinese contexts, such as in State Owned Enterprises (SOEs), are normally known as Chief Accountants (总会计师). The Chief Accountant is also addressed as "老总", that is, "Old Senior Ranking" executive. After all, "he is the one that guards the money." In the West, however, accountants are often treated as bean counters or bookkeepers.

The requirements that accountants must attain certain qualifications in order to practice in China are often viewed as employment creation. However, that is an incomplete view.

One has to understand that accounting relies tremendously on standardization and consistency, or uniformity. In a country as vast as China, not setting such practice standards and qualification requirements could give rise to chaos.

Financial Software Requirements

The financial software that is being used by an enterprise for accounting purposes must be approved by the Ministry of Finance or the local Finance Bureau. The practice and enforcement of this requirement, however, are more relaxed now. The key requirement has been that the government bureaus, such as the Tax Authority, must be able to accept the reports and returns submitted by the companies, which means that the accounting software must be compatible with the government's requirements.

Many foreign companies do not understand the rationale behind the regulations and control of accounting software. It is often seen as protectionism against foreign accounting software companies; after all in many countries outside of China, there are no restrictions on the type of accounting software to use.

The Importance of Regulating and Controlling the Use of Accounting Software

These requirements, however, are rooted in China's history. Prior to its economic opening up and reform, China was very much a centrally planned economy. In fact, central planning has been around in the Chinese culture for thousands of years. Given this history, opening up and reforming requires time and standard processes. The sheer number of companies also implies that the government needs to set certain centrally-controlled regulations for accounting codes and other matters. This will ensure that records are similar among all companies. When the Tax Authority carries out reviews from one company to another, the same account codes and detailed accounting practices will create standardization, consistency, and greater uniformity.

According to the Chinese regulations for standardization in accounting reporting, accounting code practices and external compliances must be the same throughout all companies.

The Accounting Code

The Chinese accounting code is regulated and formulated by the Ministry of Finance. All of the descriptions and coding of the chart of accounts are unified into one code.[2] In the set-up of the accounting code in the general ledger, the accounting regulations state that the first-level codes must be in accordance with the standard. The regulation provides that every company has to adopt the same first-level general ledger code.

Thus, when financial statements are submitted by various companies, a complete line item summation can be easily obtained. This makes consolidation and statistical compilation more efficient.

Many of the foreign CFOs who first visited Chinese accounting firms were very surprised when they first heard of a standard general ledger code. These codes were traditionally engraved onto small wooden pieces. When the accountant wanted to write a journal voucher, he would use the wooden pieces to imprint the codes on paper. Obviously, these have all been computerized.

So, what happens if a foreign company's home office adopts a different general ledger code? How should the company's Chinese subsidiary report to the HQ for consolidation purposes?

How Differences in the General Ledger Codes of Foreign Parent and Subsidiary Companies Are Resolved

In practice, the China subsidiary's trial balance transactions at the end of each month will have to be adjusted and mapped onto the HQ trial balance. The adjustment and mapping exercises are important steps because they link up the local subsidiary's financial statement with that of the parent company to allow for consolidation. At the same time, the group CFO at home needs to be assured that the financial statements of the local subsidiary are well prepared and supported: that is, they are tied to the original supporting entries and documents.

Regulation of Invoices

The control of the invoices ("发票," pronounced *fa piao*) is managed by the Tax Bureau. Every invoice is endorsed with a stamp that is recognized countrywide. After a company has been incorporated, it has to obtain a Tax Certificate from the Tax Bureau. Thereafter, the enterprise can request and purchase the tax invoices, also from the Taxation Bureau. The types and quantities of invoices are determined by the Taxation Bureau. Retailers, service providers, and other specialized businesses will adopt invoices related to their business types or industries. The recipient of monies from the payer must issue valid tax invoices, or *fa piaos*, to the payer. Everyone who pay for goods or services are entitled to tax invoices. Any invoices that do not comply with the requirements can be rejected by the rightful recipient.[3] A normal, valid *fa piao*, or tax invoice, should contain the following:

- The countrywide stamp for invoices
- The enterprise/organization's stamp
- The payment amount for goods or services.

The management of 发票 has been gaining greater scrutiny over time. This is especially so in major cities, such as Shanghai, Beijing, and Guangzhou, where enforcement has been very stringent.

The Purpose and Nature of *fa piao*

A *fa piao* is a necessity for deducting expenses. For example, in Shanghai and other major cities, to encourage restaurant patrons to acquire *fa piao*, the tax authority has adopted a system where *fa piao* have a silvery scratch-off portion, that once scratched, may yield a prize for the patron. The tax authority's tax revenue would obviously suffer great loss if *fa piao* were not given to patrons whenever patrons needed them.

Financial Statements

As accounting software, accounting coding, and other aspects of accounting practices are standardized and regulated, financial reporting formats should similarly be in one format.

In China, financial statements, such as profit and loss, balance sheet, and other tax filings, are all required to be in specific regulated structures. They have to be completed in every periodic cycle. Such cycles can be monthly, quarterly, or annual. Tax reporting for the company should be submitted to the Tax Bureau. These submissions form a critical part of financial reporting in China.

Proper Management of Accounting Files

The accounting files include accounting certificates, accounting books, and financial statements. These files are important records, as well as evidence that reflects the financial status of the company. The accounting archives formulated each year must be sorted and bound in compliance with relevant requirements. Companies that use accounting software to maintain accounting books should also print out an archive for preservation. According to the Regulations on Administration of Accounting Archives, the shortest period for the preservation of accounting documents and accounting books is 15 years.

Tax Adjustment on Accounting Financial Statements

For the purpose of regulating tax collection from businesses, the pretax fiscal profit of the enterprise, which is calculated in accordance with accounting standards and the accounting system, would be subject to Yearly Tax Reassessment (年度税务计算清缴). In this way, enterprise accounting is being supervised by both the Chinese financial accounting standards, as well as by national taxation laws and regulations. Under such dual supervision, differences will result from the accounting profit/loss and tax profit/loss, which make adjustments necessary. Currently, China's accounting system and taxation laws vary in several aspects.

The Differences Between China's Accounting and Tax Profit/Loss

Timing Difference

Depreciation and Amortization of Fixed and Intangible Assets

The taxation law clearly defines methods and periods for depreciation and amortization. The accounting system allows companies to decide the methods and periods that are to be adopted according to the enterprise's policies.[4] In practice, some companies may adopt the methods and periods of the tax laws to avoid confusion.

Preliminary Expense

Under the taxation law, preliminary expenses should be amortized over at least three years. However, this is different when subject to the accounting system, because preliminary expenses would be reckoned in total expenses on a one-off basis in the month when the business starts actual operations.[5]

Accrued Expense/Advance Expense

Under the taxation law, the accrued expense will only be accumulated upon actual payment,[6] while in accounting practice, it would be accrued when incurred.

Permanent Differences

(a) Expenses that are disallowed include deductions such as fines imposed for breach of laws and administrative regulations, penalties, and late payment fees.
(b) Disallowed expenses also include certain kinds of expenditures where regulated limits have been set, such as business entertainment, advertisement fees, and interest on borrowing from nonfinancial institutions.[7]

For details on the latest development in the China tax system, please refer to Chapter 6, "China's 2008 Corporate Tax Reform."

Three Issues Affecting the Chinese Accounting System

The Chinese accounting system has been developing rapidly, along with economic reform, over the last 30 years. In certain respects, the system is quite similar to Western accounting practices. This is apparent in principles and methodologies. However, the Chinese accounting system is very much influenced by governmental and administrative regulations. This is due to the need to have a common standard across the whole of China, at least as much as possible. The accounting system is also influenced by taxation laws and foreign exchange regulations. Later chapters will deal with these issues in more detail, and will discuss how currency controls influence accounting in China.

These other aspects are, in turn, influenced by the culture and history of China, despite the last 30 years of economic reforms. It is important to consider these subtle influences in order to fully appreciate the accounting system in China.

Endnotes

1. On February 15, 2007, the Ministry of Finance of the People's Republic of China promulgated the New Accounting Standards, and stated that this legislation will be first carried out in listed companies.
2. For example, see *Notice on the Printing and Distribution of Accounting Regulations for Enterprises*, promulgated by the Ministry of Finance of the People's Republic of China (CauKuai *[2000]25*号) effective January 1, 2001.
3. See Article 15, 20, 21, and 22 of the Administration Regulation on Invoices.
4. See Articles 59, 60, and 67 of the Implementation of Corporate Tax Law 2008.
5. See Article 70 of the Implementation of Corporate Tax Law 2008.
6. See Article 55 of the Implementation of Corporate Tax Law 2008.
7. See Article 37 and 43 of the Implementation of Corporate Tax Law 2008.

4

Foreign Exchange Controls

With China's economic growth requirements in mind, the Chinese Government has been carrying out restrictive policies for the inflow and outflow of foreign exchange ever since it instituted its economic reforms and open-door policy in 1978. These efforts are most apparent in the following measures:

- Effective administration of RMB foreign exchange rate to enhance the competitiveness of China's products
- Administration of the inflow and outflow of trading and nontrading foreign exchanges currencies
- Administration of foreign loans, payment of interest on foreign loans, and payment of the principal capital.

Reform of RMB Exchange Rate (1980–Present)

The reform of RMB can be divided into four stages:

1. From 1980 to 1984, a dual exchange rate system was adopted for both trade-related and non–trade-related transactions.

2. From 1985 to 1993, a dual exchange rate system, called the controlled market rate, was determined by the official exchange rate, and the foreign exchange regulation market rate was adopted.

3. From 1994 to July 20, 2005, a single, controlled and fluctuating exchange rate, based on the demand and supply of the market, was administered.

4. On July 21, 2005, a rate pegged to a basket of weighted currencies was adopted. This rate was controlled, and fluctuated in accordance with the demand and supply of the market.

In Stages 1, 2, and 3, from 1980 to July 20, 2005, the Chinese government effectively controlled the trend of the RMB exchange rate. This was especially evident during the period from 1994 to July 20, 2005, when the RMB exchange rate against the U.S. dollar was stabilized at around RMB 8.27 (as shown in Figure 4.1 below). This made Chinese-made products very competitive. It rattled all international trading partners, and they began to pressure China for an upward revaluation of RMB. Some U.S. senators even urged for a 27.5 percent punitive tariff to be imposed on China's exported products if the RMB was not revalued by 25 percent.

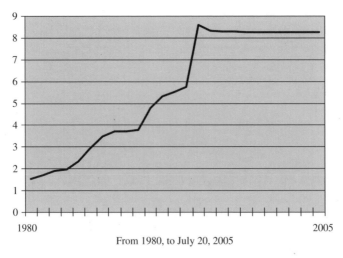

From 1980, to July 20, 2005

Figure 4.1   RMB vs. US$

Toward Implementing a Floating Exchange Rate

Under pressure from international trading partners, the Chinese government made the following announcement on July 21, 2005:

- From July 21, 2005, a managed and adjusted market rate pegged to a basket of currencies would be adopted. This rate would be managed, controlled, and fluctuated in accordance with the demand and supply of the market.
- On July 21, 2005, the US$ transaction rate against the RMB was adjusted, and it was announced that it would start at US$ 1 to RMB 8.11. This would mean that the RMB had been revalued by 2 percent (from 8.27).

The Exchange Rate Trend between RMB and the U.S. Dollar Since 2005

Since July 21, 2005, the RMB has been experiencing gradual and slow upward revaluation. At the end of 2005, it had risen to RMB 8.07 to US$ 1. At the end of 2006, it had been revalued to RMB 7.81 to US$ 1. Figure 4.2 illustrates this trend.[1]

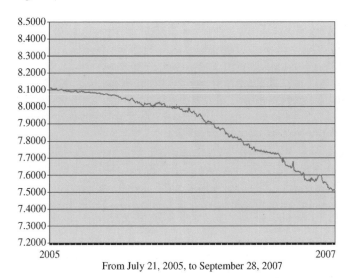

From July 21, 2005, to September 28, 2007

Figure 4.2   Medium RMB vs. US$ Market Rate

Various Types of Foreign Currency Accounts for Foreign Investors in China

Foreign Investors and Enterprises in China

Where a foreign investor does not establish a foreign-invested enterprise (FIE), but engages in specific direct investment projects or activities (项目) related to direct investment within the territory of China, he or she may apply to the State Administration of Foreign Exchange (SAFE) at the place of the investment project to open a designated foreign exchange bank account in his or her own name.

A foreign investor is only allowed to open a multicurrency designated foreign exchange account in one bank, unless otherwise approved by the foreign exchange bureau. Such an account may be classified into four types according to its function:

1. **Investment Account** Where a foreign investor carries out contracted projects, cooperative exploitation, development and exploration of resources, and engages in venture capital within the territory of China, he or she may apply to open such an account. He or she will need to obtain the nonindependent legal representative (非独立法人代表) business license for depositing and paying the relevant foreign exchange funds.

2. **Purchase Account** Where a foreign investor intends to establish a foreign-invested enterprise (FIE) within the territory of China, and needs to purchase the land use rights and immovable property attached thereto, machinery and equipment, or other assets, and so forth at the preliminary stage, he or she may apply to open such an account for depositing and paying foreign exchange purchases. These processes are to be carried out after the asset purchase contracts come into effect.

3. **Expense Account** When a foreign investor that intends to establish a foreign-invested enterprise (FIE) within the territory of China needs to conduct such work as market research and planning, preparation of an institutional establishment, and so forth at the preliminary stage, he or she may apply to open such an account (temporary bank account) for depositing and paying the relevant foreign exchange funds after obtaining the Notice of Preliminary Approval of Enterprise Name issued by the State Administration of Industry and Commerce Department (SAIC).

FICE

A U.S. company in the business of furniture trading decided to establish a foreign investor commercial enterprise (FICE) subsidiary in Shanghai. In the beginning, the parent company incurred costs and expenses for market research, planning, rental deposits, and so forth. It mistakenly believed that these costs could later become part of the investment capital in the subsidiary. The parent company failed to set up the temporary bank account to disburse the expenses at the initial stage. Hence upon setting up and acquisition of the business license, the company was still required to inject full capital.

In this case study, if the company had adopted the procedures as described in Item 3, "Expense Account," the amount of invested capital could have been reduced by the expensed amount. It is also important to note that the expenses paid out from the temporary account have to be approved by the SAFE.

After obtaining the Approval Letter for the enterprise's name registration, the enterprise can apply for a temporary account for its daily expenses. However, such accounts are strictly limited. Foreign investors are only entitled to open one account at one bank for the use of multiple currency transactions. The account's ceiling, period, and expense limits must be checked and ratified by the State Administration of Foreign Exchange (SAFE) upon the opening of the account. The SAFE is also in charge of the daily administration of the account. The foreign investor's funds in this account must be remitted in the form of bank transfers, instead of cash deposits. Each settlement and transfer shall be first approved by the SAFE. The funds in the account must not be used directly to make disbursements to the foreign invested enterprises.

This is why the SAFE applies such strict controls, which can deter investors from opening such "temporary bank accounts." Normally, the SAFE would only approve expenses incurred at the point of the establishment of the subsidiary. Market study expenses such as trip expenses, and so forth are normally considered costs of the parent company, which should not be taken from part of the future capital of the subsidiary.

Money Matters

In the previous example, the parent company remitted monies from overseas to pay the rental deposit and renovation expenses. These were later recorded as accounts owing to the parent company, since they could not form part of the capital of the subsidiary. However, the procedures were incomplete, and the funds could not be repaid to the parent company in foreign currency. In the future, if the parent company incurs expenses in China, it will be able to request that the subsidiary pay in RMB. This is probably one way to "repay" the amount owing to the parent company.

Guarantee Account

Where a foreign investor needs to provide guarantee of funds to a domestic institution in accordance with the relevant provisions and the agreements in a contract before making investments within the territory of China, it may, within the time limit set out in the contracts, apply to open such an account for depositing and paying foreign exchange guarantee funds. When a foreign investor applies to open a designated foreign exchange account, it must submit to the local territory's SAFE Bureau with materials that can prove the authenticity and legitimacy of its investment activities. The foreign exchange bureau will verify matters such as the maximum limit, duration, and scope of the income and expenditure of the relevant account, and conduct daily supervision. The funds in the designated foreign exchange account of the foreign investor will be remitted by spot foreign exchange instead of cash. The settlement and transfer of the exchange funds in the account must be verified and approved by the foreign exchange bureau on a per amount basis.

Capital Verification

After the incorporation of foreign invested enterprises, the balance of foreign exchange accounts for the foreign investor can be transferred into the capital account. The capital verifications must be performed on the capital account. Written authorization issued by the State Administration of Foreign Exchange will serve as documentary support. In the case where the foreign invested enterprise is not established in China, the investor can proceed with the purchase and remittance of unused capital, as well as outward remittance with related written authorization issued by the SAFE.

In Summation

A Singapore parent company in the business of consulting set up a subsidiary in Shanghai. The paid-up or registered capital to be injected into the subsidiary was US$ 140,000. Then, the parent company decided to make it US$ 140,050 instead. The additional US$ 50 was meant to cover the bank remittance costs. Upon receipt of the money, the SAFE disapproved the injection, citing that the amount injected was not as approved under the business license. The company was required to remit the amount back to the parent company, and reinject the exact amount of capital.

In this case study, the investor company should have noted that only the exact approved amount could be injected. The related expenses and costs would then be accounted for separately in the accounts of the subsidiary. This procedure is exactly as the SAFE stipulates.

Bank Accounts for Foreign Individuals

Foreign individuals can open personal deposit accounts that include a personal savings account, and a personal debt settlement account. A valid passport must be produced by foreign individuals to qualify for the application. The personal debt settlement account includes the personal checking account, debit card account and credit card account. Foreign investors only need to provide the account number, name of the owner, and the name of the bank to the remitter where a foreign capital inflow is required.

For salaries in RMB and rightful earnings after taxes, foreign individuals can convert them into foreign exchange from authorized banks with proof that taxes have been paid. No withdrawals are permitted. They can remit the foreign exchange (after conversion) back to his accounts in the home countries.

Salaries, bonuses, and allowances for foreign employees cannot be delivered in the form of foreign cash directly; however, these can be remitted both ways from the enterprise's foreign exchange account to the employee's personal foreign exchange deposit account.

The foreigner should submit his or her written application, valid passport or proof of identity, employment contract (including work certificate issued by the Labor Bureau, or expert certificate issued by the State Administration of Foreign Affairs, together with the employment contract), RMB income list and proof that taxes have been paid, along with the designated bank account in order to obtain foreign exchange and proceed with outward remittance.

Foreign Debt

Foreign debt refers to debts in foreign currency owed by domestic institutions to nonresidents. *Domestic institutions* refer to permanent establishments within China, which include, but are not limited to government agencies, domestic financial institutions, enterprises, public institutions, and social organizations. *Nonresidents* refer to institutions and natural persons outside China, and nonpermanent institutions legally established in China.

The Investment Differential

The total sum of the medium- and long-term foreign debts, and the total sum of the short-term foreign debt balance must be controlled within the difference between the total investment and the registered capital approved by the authority. The difference between the total investment figure and the registered capital is normally known as the "investment differential." Within these limits, the foreign invested enterprise may take out foreign loans. For any part exceeding this difference, the total investment must be increased by resubmission of an application to the authorities for examination and approval.

Medium- and long-term foreign debts must be used strictly in accordance with approved means, and are not allowed to be appropriated for other uses. If it becomes necessary to use debts for other purposes, an application shall be submitted, and will follow the usual routine approval processes by authorities. Short-term foreign debts must be used mainly as liquid cash. Such debts cannot be used for medium- and long-term applications, for example, investment in fixed assets.

Management of Foreign Currency Debt for Foreign Invested Enterprises (Certain Special Types of FIEs)

1. For foreign invested enterprises of which the foreign investor's equity contribution is less than 25 percent, the incurrence of debt shall be in accordance with relative regulations that apply to domestic Chinese invested enterprises.

2. In the case where the foreign enterprise's approved total investment equals the registered capital, or the total investment is not determined, the enterprise should file the new registered capital amount with the authorities for reapproval. The principle of "difference between total investment and registered capital, or the investment differential concept shall be applied to the debt incurred."

3. The investment scale of a company controlled by a foreign investor shall be managed in accordance with the following rules: for enterprises with registered capital that is not lower than US$ 30 million, the summation of the short-term foreign debt balance and the accumulated amount of medium- and long-term debts shall not be more than four times the paid-up registered capital. For those of which the registered capital is not less than US$ 100 million, the summation must not be more than six times the paid-up registered capital.

4. The total amount of risk assets of a foreign invested leasing company is defined as

   $$\text{total amount of risk assets} = \text{total assets} - \text{cash} - \text{cash in bank}$$
   $$- \text{government bonds} - \text{leased assets}$$

5. This shall not exceed 10 times the total amount of its net assets. The company's assets derived from external debt incurred must all be categorized as risky assets.

6. When dealing with domestic debt incurred under overseas guarantees, such as guarantees from the parent company, the amount must fall under the external foreign currency debt controlled by the SAFE under the same regulations.

7. When a foreign multinational company conducts the centralized management of capital and foreign exchange funds within the group, the capital absorbed by the multinational company that is used onshore by overseas-affiliated companies should be regarded as external foreign currency debts for management.

Administration Procedures for the Arrangement of a Foreign Currency Loan

When an FIE decides to obtain a foreign currency loan, for instance, from its parent entity, it should strictly follow the necessary administrative procedures regulated under the SAFE. First, the FIE should sign a Foreign Debt Contract with the overseas entity. Thereafter, it should provide the Foreign Debt Contract, along with other required documents, to the SAFE within 15 days. After reviewing, the SAFE will issue the Registration Certificate for Foreign Debt to the FIE if the Foreign Debt Contract has complied with all the necessary regulations.

With the Registration Certificate for Foreign Debt, the FIE should open a Foreign Debt Account in the bank. The foreign debt can only be remitted to the Foreign Debt Account. Every month, the FIE should complete the tax filing of withholding business tax and withholding enterprise income tax with the Tax Authority for the interest payable on the foreign debt. When the FIE pays the interest and repays the principal amount, it should also obtain the relevant approval from the SAFE.

The Importance of Investment Differential

The total sum of the accumulated amount of the enterprise's medium- and long-term foreign debt, and the balance of short-term foreign debt must be strictly controlled within the difference between the approved total investment and the registered capital. The SAFE will neither register nor ratify the foreign exchange settlement of the excess amount of the foreign invested enterprise's remittance unless the change of capital has been approved by the original approval authority. If the excess amount has been remitted, the enterprise should apply to the original approval authority for ratification of change of total investment. In such a case, the SAFE will permit the applicant to keep the foreign debt for three months and after that, the excess amount will have to be remitted back to its origin.

When proceeding with the check and ratification of a foreign invested enterprise's capital and external debt transaction, the SAFE and designated foreign exchange banks would request the enterprise to provide written authorization for payment whenever there is a

---

Unsafe Practice

A European parent company in the business of cable manufacturing decided to assist its China subsidiary in working capital funding. It was ill advised by the local staff that it could simply verify the foreign currency as a loan to its subsidiary. It did not go through the procedures as mentioned above. Upon remittance, the SAFE considered those receipts as "revenue" of the subsidiary. The latter had to pay business taxes at five percent. Moreover, the parent could not receive "repayment" of the loan.

---

one-off transaction of more than US$ 200,000, in addition to conducting routine checks and ratifications as required by law. For salary payments, retained petty cash, and settlement capital of less than US$ 200,000 in value, written authorization may not be required. However, when the enterprise goes for the next transaction, a list of uses for the funds should be provided. The foreign debt transaction cannot be used for repayments of debts in RMB.

Interactions Between Foreign Currency Controls and Taxation

Due to regulations in foreign currency and taxation in China, many foreign currency transactions by foreign businesses inevitably have to deal with taxation. The two are so intertwined that the State Administration of Foreign Exchange, the Tax Authorities, and the banks are largely in close communication. Taxation of foreign exchange transactions is mainly performed in the following situations, which are known as "external payment under nontrading items":

Pursuant to the Chinese Tax Law, a five percent business tax, and a 10 percent enterprise income tax (EIT) or individual income tax (IIT) should be paid within the territory of China before the non-trade foreign exchange payment occurs. In respect of non-trade foreign exchange payment that does not include IIT, the average rate is 14.5 percent.

$$[5\% \text{ business tax} + (1 - 5\%) * 10\% \text{ EIT}]$$

Whenever a domestic institution or an individual obtains foreign exchange for payment or conducts a related outward payment from the foreign exchange account with a foreign-exchange–designated bank, proofs of payment for related business taxes, EIT, or IIT, which are issued by tax authorities, and tax receipts must be submitted to the authority.

- Incomes of enterprises and individuals outside China include those that are directly engaged in architecture, installation, surveillance, construction, transportation, decoration, maintenance, design, debugging, consultancy, auditing, training, agency management, and contracted projects. In this context, *direct engagement* is defined as fulfillment of contracts or agreements.
- For certain foreign investors without establishments in China, certain income items when remitted as foreign currency back home from China will be excluded from business tax. The list of items includes interest, guarantee fees, rental fees, disclosure fees (inclusive of patent rights, nonpatent rights, trade mark rights, copyrights, and brand name/goodwill), property transfer income, equity transfer earnings, land use rights transfer income, and so on. According to the current tax law, for the aforesaid interest items, guarantee fee items, rental fees (apart from rental of real estate), income from property transfer (apart from transfer of real estate) in a property transfer, and income from equity transfer are exempted from business tax; thus, there is no need to submit proofs of tax payment of business income, and invoices in these situations.

Foreign Currency Employment Income and Tax Thereon

According to the current tax law, IIT is levied on salaries and payments to foreign employees, Chinese employees with overseas permanent residential permits, and employees from Hong Kong, Macau, and Taiwan employed by domestic institutions (including those paid via the parent company of the employee). For these remunerations, business tax is not imposed. When obtaining foreign funds or outward payments from the foreign exchange account, proofs of payment of IIT and tax receipts issued by local tax authorities must be submitted.

Multinationals Payment of Nontrade Items to Foreign Employees

Minimum Wage
An overseas company was intending to pay wages of foreign employees for a foreign invested company from outside China. Although relevant proof of tax payment was available, the remittance was prohibited under regulations of foreign exchange control.

According to the Circular of the State Administration of Foreign Exchange on the Management of Collection and Sales of Nontrade Foreign Exchange of Transnational Companies (Hui Fa [2004] No. 62), multinational corporations are allowed to examine and approve the process of obtaining nontrading exchanges if the following conditions are met:

- *Multinational corporations* refer to enterprise groups that own affiliated companies both at home and overseas, with one affiliated company within the territory of China that exercises the group's function of global or regional (including China) investment management. This is inclusive of both Chinese invested multinational corporations, and foreign invested multinational corporations.
- If multinational corporations and their domestic affiliated companies, pay salaries, benefits and allowances for foreign and Hong Kong and Macau employees or employees of Chinese nationality but possessing permanent overseas residential rights (hereinafter referred to as foreign employees) that have been paid by overseas headquarters or overseas affiliate companies, or remit overseas the salaries, benefits, and allowances for foreign employees, the overseas payment notices, ID certification of foreign employees such as passports, and employment certification such as labor contracts, and tax certification and other evidentiary materials may be held for payment from the foreign exchange accounts or purchase of foreign exchanges with RMB at the designated banks of foreign exchanges.
- The above-mentioned multinational corporations and their domestic affiliate companies must be checked and ratified by the local Administration of Foreign Exchange, and then be filed with the SAFE for purpose of recording.

- For multinational corporations that do not fulfill the above requirements, but that are free from major violations of regulations in the last three years, have abided by the foreign exchange administration, are in a good financial situation, with a large volume of foreign exchange payments under current accounts, and with important local influences (the foreign investor's actual contribution must not be less than 25 percent) may also handle the sales and payment of nontrade foreign exchange according to the provisions of the circular with approval by the local competent foreign exchange administration. Also, the local Administration of Foreign Exchange will file a list of the above-mentioned nonmultinational companies with the SAFE.

From the above conditions, we can see that if the foreign invested enterprise wants to pay overseas salaries, benefits, and allowance for foreign employees, it has to file an application with the local Administration of Foreign Exchange. The legal ground for such approval is the Circular of the State Administration of Foreign Exchange on the Management of Collection and Sales of Nontrade Foreign Exchange of Transnational Companies (Hui Fa [2004] No. 62).

Tax Exemption for Certain Foreign Currency Payments

For certain foreign currency income items, the SAFE and Tax Authority, in particular, do provide for tax exemption. For example, for items listed below, corporate income tax (or individual income tax) can be exempted, according to the current tax law of China and relevant regulations. However, domestic institutions or personnel who purchase foreign exchange for payments, or pay outwards from their foreign exchange accounts must provide tax exemption documents issued by the Tax Authority, as well as other materials as required by the authority:

- Royalty fees obtained by the foreign enterprise for providing exclusive technology for China's scientific research, resource exploration, traffic development, agricultural/forest/husbandry activities, and development of important techniques.
- Bond interest paid to overseas bond holders by domestic Chinese invested financial institutions, and enterprises issuing these bonds outside China.

- Interest on loans provided by financial institutions or banks, and companies that are designated in tax treaties between China and the other countries.
- Interest from loans to the China Bank that are provided by overseas banks on a preferential rate basis.
- Where domestic institutions purchase technology, equipment, and goods from overseas, and where the foreign seller's bank is providing the credit, the domestic institution's payment of the interest (when such interest is paid at rates not exceeding China buyer's bank's rate) will be exempted from tax.
- Interest obtained by the foreign enterprises when Chinese domestic institutions purchase technologies and equipment, and where the total principal and interest are paid to these foreign enterprises by means of goods provision (such as product buy-back and delivery of goods), or by offsetting the assembly fee for the processing of the materials supplied by Chinese domestic institutions. This interest is exempted from tax.
- Interest included in lease fees charged by lessor companies outside China for the provision of equipment to users in China via financial leasing. This interest rate should not be higher than the export credit rate of the country of the lessor.
- Other situations that can be tax-exempted according to tax treaties China has with other countries (regions) as cited in relevant laws and regulations.

In addition to the above, where the following situations occur, taxes may not be levied or are exempted, when the company purchases foreign currency or makes payments from the foreign exchange account. However the tax-exemption proofs (or tax-paid proofs if already paid) must be presented to the Tax Authority.

- Dividends: Where foreign enterprises and enterprises that issue B shares[2] issue shares outside China, the dividend distributed after the payment of income tax based on business profit is tax exempted. When buying foreign currencies or outward payments from foreign exchange accounts occur, tax-paid proof (pertaining to the profit that has been distributed as dividends), which is issued by the tax authority (certified by the tax authority) or relevant resolution of Board of Directors on dividend distribution must be provided.

- Please note the following list of items: service fees, brokerage charges, commission fees that are incurred outside China, such as advertising fees, upkeep fees, design fees, consulting fees, and training fees. According to the principle of "territorial jurisdiction" in China's income tax regulations, the abovementioned services incurred outside China will not be taxable. However, if the payment is required to be made to a foreign party, there is still a need to provide a certificate, or proof, or non-levy from the Tax Authority in making such payments.
- For interest derived by the foreign government from loans to the Chinese government, and the national bank of China, such interest is exempted. Under the current tax law of China, tax proofs issued by the authority need not be provided.
- Relevant tax proofs of the following capital-related incomes must be submitted to the State Administration of Foreign Exchange, or its branches five days before domestic institutions or individuals purchase foreign currencies, or conduct payments from their foreign exchange bank accounts, as stipulated in the regulations. Designated banks will proceed with the purchases and payments of foreign exchanges after the examination and approval by the SAFE, or its branches when they can produce proof of the written authorization.
  - Direct debt interest (excluding loan interests provided by foreign governments)
  - Guarantee fees
  - Financing lease fees
  - Income from transfer of real estate
  - Interest from equity transfer

Conclusion

Despite the opening up and economic reforms in China, foreign exchange transactions are still under very strict government control. The Chinese government still believes that strong foreign exchange control is good for the entire national economy. With continuous globalization and greater participation of foreign investors in the Chinese economy, it is still necessary to have a strong hold on foreign currencies moving in and out of as China, as well as within. China will continue to manage foreign exchange for the following key reasons:

- For macroeconomic regulation and stability
- To prevent large sums of overseas capital from flooding China's market
- To preserve and increase the value of the country's foreign exchanges

With the huge trade surplus built over the years, China's foreign exchange reserves have also been rising. At the end of 2007, they hit a record of US$ 1.5 trillion. The continuing growth of foreign exchange reserves has caused nations around the world to pressure the Chinese government for the upward revaluation of the RMB. It is estimated that the exchange rate of RMB to US$ will continue to appreciate. Up to the end of January 2008, the US$ to RMB was US$ 1 to RMB 7.19. It will probably pass the point of RMB 7, to potentially below RMB 7, perhaps to RMB 6.5 to US$ 1 in the near future.

The RMB upward revaluation will bring great pressure to China's economy, especially since China's current economic growth is mainly driven by fixed asset investments, and the government's efforts to increase international exports over the past 30 years. The revaluation of RMB will augment China's inflation. In particular, China's economy has been growing for several years at double-digit rates, and a trend of serious economic overheating has already emerged. It is predicted that China will continue with strict foreign exchange controlling policies.

However, as China becomes more closely involved in economic globalization, the current foreign exchange system will no longer be adequate for a more sophisticated economic situation. It should be a priority for China to reform the foreign exchange policy system in consideration of the continuous opening up of the economy. China should make strategic plans for globalization in order to create a flexible and effective framework for the system.

At present, the Chinese government has already loosened the foreign exchange control over individuals' capital, while the reform of foreign exchange control over foreign capital will be further accelerated and implemented on a wider scale. However, in an effort to stabilize the financial situation in China, no large-scale changes will be made in the short term. Many believe that the Chinese government will continue to loosen the foreign exchange control slowly and gradually, to explore and establish a set of foreign exchange administration policies that meet the needs of new developments for China and the world.

Endnotes

1. The latest exchange rate on August 28, 2008 is 6.83 RMB to 1 US$ (http://www.boc.cn/en/common/service, Bank of China Information Center, July 28, 2008).
2. B shares: these involve companies incorporated in mainland China and are traded in the mainland B-share markets (Shanghai and Shenzhen). B shares are quoted in foreign currencies. In the past, only foreigners were allowed to trade B shares. Starting from March 2001, mainlanders can trade B shares as well. However, they must trade with legal foreign currency accounts.

5

Taxation

The Myth of the Chinese Tax System

Many businesses fail to understand the Chinese tax system. They believe that China is so big that there is no system that applies universally across the country. In fact, many have thought that China has different tax systems across provinces and cities. Such incorrect beliefs come from stories, hearsay, and myths.

The Tax System Is Actually Unified

China has a sophisticated tax system, and the country, as a whole, follows one tax system. The tax laws are formulated at the state level. The National People's Congress (NPC) debates and votes on the various tax bills submitted. Once voted and passed, the State Council will gazette it into a law, signed by the president. This law will then be administered and enforced by the State Administration of Taxation (SAT). The SAT administers the law by handing down the laws and tax regulations to the various tax authorities in the provinces, federal territories, and cities.

Due to the vastness of China, and because implementation involves various levels of bureaucracy, tax regulations frequently can be interpreted and administered differently in different places. Enforcement of the unified Tax Law varies because of the different interpretation and treatments at local tax authorities.

A Brief Overview of the Taxation Administration Structure in China

Figure 5.1 below indicates that tax law formulated at the state level will be implemented through the various levels of jurisdiction. One can also expect the same administrative structure in other government functions.

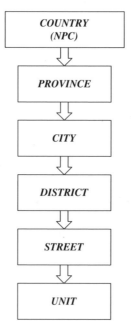

Figure 5.1   China's Taxation Administration Structure

Figure 5.2 shows the tax administrative structure and system are enforced within the local authority. In a locality such as Shanghai, the local tax structure can be fairly complex. Within this structure, there are various units. Each of them will be in charge of different functions.

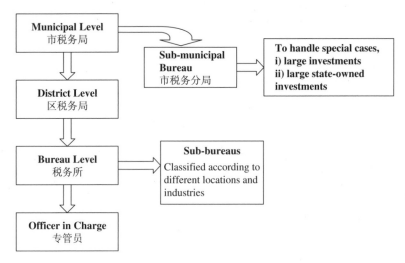

Figure 5.2 Typical Tax Administration and Enforcement Structure

Latest Corporate Tax Reform, Effective January 1, 2008

The latest corporate tax law was adopted on March 16 2007, effective January 1, 2008.

Transition in the Chinese Government's Stand Toward Attracting Foreign Investments

The main principle of the new tax law is to establish a level playing field between local and foreign companies operating in China. It has been almost 30 years since China opened its doors under the economic reform launched by Deng Xiaoping in 1978. In order to attract foreign direct investments (FDI), China has given preferential tax treatment to many foreign investors. In the last five years, there have been great lobbying efforts by local enterprises to the Chinese government for fairer treatment between local and foreign companies. This lobby has been gaining great momentum since China joined the World Trade Organisation (WTO) in December 2001. This has led to the formulation of corporate tax reform. All companies, whether local or foreign (with few exceptions), will pay a tax rate of 25 percent effective January 1, 2008. Foreign companies that have had tax holidays previously will have a five-year transition treatment to consume and fully utilize the tax holiday. Chapter 6 will provide detailed guidance to CFOs in the discussion of the 2008 Corporate Tax Reform.

Types of Taxes

Besides having a tax implementation and enforcement structure, China has various types of taxes classified within the categories of State Tax (国税) and Local Tax (地税). The revenues of state taxes go to the state coffers. The revenues of local taxes go to the coffers of local governments (for example, city, federal territory, or province) for local usage.

State and Land Taxes

Examples of state taxes include

- Value Added Tax (增值税)
- Corporate Income Tax (企业所得税)
- Custom Tax (关税)
- Vehicle Purchase Tax (车辆购置税)

Examples of land taxes include

- Business Tax (营业税)
- Individual Income Tax (个人所得税)
- Property Tax (房产税)
- Stamp Duty (印花税)

Tax Rates Are Similar Throughout the Country

As mentioned above, when a tax law is passed, the tax rates are implemented across the entire country. Local tax authorities at the local government are not allowed to change the tax rates (with the exception of certain state-approved locations).

The Myth of Lower Tax Rates

Many times, we have come across rumors from businessmen who have travelled to certain China cities to invest. They are very prone to believe, after a conversation with the local investment officer, that they are entitled to a certain low tax rate (for example, a Corporate Income Tax rate that is lower than the current 33 percent).

Financial Subsidies Are in Place

Such beliefs are generally incorrect. Local investment officers cannot alter the tax rates set by the state. Local investment officers can, however, offer financial subsidies to attract Foreign Direct Investments (FDIs) into their zones. These financial subsidies are granted to induce foreign investors to invest in certain locations. Such entities are still required to pay taxes like any other enterprises, but they get a refund from the local government later.

The local government is able to do this because the subsidy comes from its own budget.

The collection and distribution of state taxes are illustrated in Figure 5.3. A predetermined portion of these revenues is kept by the state, with the rest being distributed to the various provinces. The provincial government will then use the provincially determined rate to distribute the tax collection from the state to the various cities. Similarly, the city officials will distribute a certain percentage to its various districts.

Land Tariff Need Not Be Given to State

Land tax collection is implemented in the same way as the state tax distribution. The only difference is that the provincial government has complete autonomy over the distribution of the local tax collection, and none of it needs to be handed over to the state government.

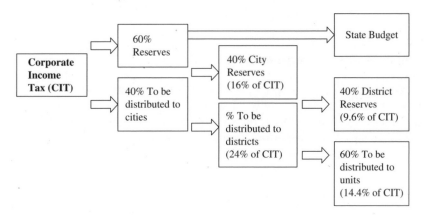

Figure 5.3 Where Do the Revenues Go?

Where the Financial Subsidy Comes From

Financial subsidies are normally apportioned out of the local provincial budget, some of which is derived from the collection of local taxes. If the Foreign Investment Enterprise pays a certain level of business taxes, it will be entitled to some financial subsidy, which is derived from the district fiscal budget. It is to be noted that qualifying for financial subsidies does not mean that the business tax is no longer applicable.

Duty Calls

A company wanted to establish an entity in Guangzhou. It was told by the local Business Promotion Bureau that if it paid business taxes above a certain level, it would be entitled to "certain reduced tax rates." Being new and unclear about the functionality of financial subsidies, the company perceived that it would not need to pay the business tax. As a result, it did not pay the mandatory business tax and, of course, incurred unnecessary penalties.

The company should pay the business tax of five percent as it normally would. At the end of the period (depending on the local agreement), the company can then submit an application for a financial subsidy. The company needs to sign a written agreement for this to be effective.

A Levy Is Not the Same as a Tax

There is another item called a levy. Levies are not taxes or financial subsidies. They are normally social responsibility contributions to the district or locality in which the foreign entity operates. Normally, levies occur at the "district/county/street" levels. They are collected by the local street council. One example is the City Development Levy (城市建设维护税). The levy is paid to the local street council, and the proceeds can be used to develop the street. Taxes and levies are conceptually different although from the foreign investor's point of view, their effect may be quite similar.

The City Development Levy can be calculated as follows:

(VAT + Consumption Tax + Business Tax) × 0.5%

The Concept of Tax Incentives

Ever since China adopted an open door policy in the 1980s, foreign direct investments in China have been increasing tremendously. To stimulate the domestic economy, and at the same time attract more foreign investments, China has introduced an array of tax incentives. The initial phase of the policy was directed at the coastal regions, including such cities as Zhuhai, Shenzhen, and Guangzhou. In recent years, areas in the Yangtze Delta Region have also benefited from these policies.

Tax incentives may take the form of:

- Reduced tax rates
- Tax exemption and tax holiday periods
- Tax refunds on reinvested profits
- Other tax incentives

Foreign Enterprises Need to Apply for Tax Incentives

These tax incentives are available to all foreign enterprises, but this does not mean that the enterprises will automatically receive them. Applications must be submitted by the foreign enterprises to the local tax authorities for approval. If the approval authority is not within that level's jurisdiction, the application needs to be passed on to a higher hierarchical level, level by level, for approval.

Preferential Treatment Is Not Automatically Granted

When first investing in this project, the foreign investor was "promised" that the "five-year tax holiday, five-year half-tax" would be "granted" by the state due to the sheer size of investment commitment.

This tax incentive is an available incentive, and is in accordance with preferential treatment policies. However, the foreign investor did nothing further to establish the entity; believing that "nothing further needed to be done."

5/5

In the case of a major foreign investor's investment in an infrastructure project, the foreign enterprise thought that the preferential "five-year tax exemption, five-year tax reduction" (5/5 tax incentive policy) would be granted automatically. However, this was later understood not to be so.

The 5/5 tax incentive policy stipulates that investment in ports and shipyard constructions enjoys the "five-year tax holiday, five-year half tax" policy. The average rate is 15 percent. In Shanghai Pudong New Area and Hainan Province, all the infrastructure projects of more than 15 years also get to enjoy the incentive at an average rate of 7.5 percent. In Hainan Province, investments involved in development and management of agriculture also enjoy the incentive, at an average rate of 7.5 percent.

Need to Apply to the Authority

In fact, the entity needs to make its application with the Local Bureau of the Ministry of Commerce, and the local tax authority. The application was eventually made and flowed to the municipal level, provincial level, and finally to the state level. About one year after the entity was set up, the foreign invested enterprise received the tax exemption certificate.

With the new Corporate Tax reform, several of the tax preferential treatment and policies have been abolished.

Incentives Will Be Focused Toward Specific Industries

Although the Chinese government continues to welcome FDIs, it is directing more focus toward high technology, environmentally friendly, and industrially safe products. Hence, tax incentives will be given to these industries. The focus, with a few exceptions, is no longer based upon location or investment zones.

Tax Compliance

When a foreign entity invests in China, one of the most important issues is that it must be consistently "tax compliant." Many business people do not understand the due processes within the framework of tax compliance. Failure on one or two processes may lead to serious consequences. The following illustrates certain key compliances processes.

Tax Registration Is Not Automatic

Many people assume that their enterprises will automatically be registered with the Tax Authority if their application is approved by the Ministry of Commerce. This is unfortunately not the whole story. Upon receiving approval from the Ministry of Commerce, a business entity must apply to register for tax with the local Tax Bureau. The tax authority will award local and state tax certificates to the entity once it is registered for tax purposes.

Tax Rate Determination Is a Mandatory Process

In addition to the above, the entity is still not ready to pay taxes. It has to submit and confirm its tax certificates with the tax officer in charge. The latter will determine the types of taxes the entity needs to file periodically, and at which tax rates it will be charged. This is called Tax Rate Determination (税务核定).

Prompt Submission Can Be Challenging

The enterprise will also have to be responsible for prompt submission of tax returns. Submission of returns can normally be a very complicated process. As discussed, there are various types of taxes and different rates that may apply. Deadlines for the submission of the different taxes differ, which make tax compliance even more challenging. The following illustrates the timing of tax returns submission:

- Business Taxes—Monthly
- Value Added Taxes—Monthly

- Individual Income Taxes—Monthly and yearly if the annual income exceeds RMB 120,000
- Corporate Income Taxes—Quarterly and yearly tax assessment

Penalties/Late Payment Charges: Authorities Are Very Strict

The Chinese government is very strict about being tax compliant. They take a very firm stand that enterprises comply with the taxation laws. Failure to do so can result in heavy fines. The company that fails to pay taxes promptly may be exposed to penalties, besides having to pay the delinquent taxes. In addition, the Tax Authority can also impose late payment charges. The system in major cities in China is electronically controlled. So if taxes are not paid up, the taxpayer company's file will remain open. The penalties and late payment charges will accumulate.

Cases where the Authorities May Allow Backfiling

Despite the tough view taken by the authorities, if good relationships are maintained with the Tax Authorities, backfiling may be possible.

Owning Up

A foreign investor had several expatriates working in an FIE that was incorporated in Shanghai. The expatriates did not have any idea of the individual income tax system, and thus did not pay any income tax for the income they received in China. It was only after almost a year that they discovered that they were not income tax compliant as individuals.

Consultants were called in to unwind the situation. Initially, the tax authorities wanted to be very strict on this issue. The consultants assisted in explaining to the authorities that the issue of noncompliance was genuinely a case of ignorance, and that the expatriates had sincerely owned up to the mistake. The authorities sympathized with the company, and waived the penalty after quite a bit of effort by the consultants.

In the above example, the FIE has to withhold the monthly individual income taxes of the employees and submit them to the Tax Authority monthly.

Tax Liquidation

Many businesses that start out in China cannot expect that all their efforts will successful. If the company fails, it will need to cease operations and be liquidated.

Always Choose the Right Location from the Start

Sometimes, an entity that is operating in one location needs to move to another. In China, it is more complex to make such moves, because of the sheer size of the country. For instance, in Shanghai, there are probably 20 district tax authorities. This might require deregistration in one district tax authority, and reregistration in another. If a company is liquidating, it must realize that liquidation in the China context can be

---

From A to B

A Registered Office (RO) wants to move from District A to District B.

At the time when the RO was set up in District A, the managers mistakenly believed that it would be quite easy to move from A to B when they needed to do so. So in fact when they first set up, they registered A in a service center. They never intended to stay there for long. Their intentions were to move to a bigger office when things became more stable.

The client's attorney went straight to deregister the RO from A to B with the local district's Investment Authorities. However, District A's tax authorities did not wish to let the RO be deregistered as a taxpayer under its jurisdiction. After all, the RO was contributing substantial tax revenue to A.

Consultants managed to unwind the process by getting District A's tax authority to process the tax deregistration first. In addition, at the onset of the RO's operation, the consultants had ensured a good tax compliance by the RO. This helped substantially.

very laborious. The most laborious part of the liquidation process is tax liquidation. We will discuss liquidation in greater detail in the final chapter, "Closing A Business in China."

Authorities Dislike Tax Deregistration

Most local tax authorities dislike tax liquidation because it means a loss of tax revenue for them. Therefore, enterprises that begin tax liquidation must be very careful to ensure compliance with tax regulations, and follow administrative processes.

A Company Intends to Move Elsewhere at a Later Stage

The above example demonstrates that getting the sequencing wrong and not ensuring good compliance practice could have been disastrous to the entire tax liquidation process.

Tax Liquidation Calls for Various Processes

Tax liquidation normally calls for various administration processes; the completion of applications, the submission of reviews, and approval. It also requires reviews and approval by the various units of the local tax authority, including the officer in charge and the policy review unit, as well as a tax audit by the inspection unit.

Building Relationships: *Guanxi* Plays a Huge Role in China

Guanxi (关系), is literally defined as "relationship." It is a term almost synonymous with doing business in China, and it plays an integral part of dealing with the Tax Authorities here. Consultants normally encourage their clients to build a very good relationship with their Tax Officer and the subordinates whom they deal with.

Building the Right Relationships

Building relationships with the right people is very important. This will normally be a determining factor in many business dealings in China.

Guanxi

One of the FIEs did almost everything correctly but did not build a good relationship with the Tax Officer's subordinate. As a result, when the Tax Officer stepped down and his subordinate took over, the subordinate (now the new Tax Officer) took the opportunity to make things difficult for the FIE, since he felt neglected. He created difficulties whenever the FIE needed to carry out any tax processes with the authorities. The FIE should have been more proactive by discussing and consulting the subordinate in most matters. *Guanxi* or building relationships is a very important, but often a forgotten part of dealing with taxation authorities in China.

Taxation in China

A successful CFO must thoroughly understand local taxation laws and requirements. Taking the right approach and handling issues the best way can translate into essential benefits for your organization.

6

China's 2008 Corporate Tax Reform

Since the start of the economic reform 30 years ago, China has undergone major taxation changes and developments. However, it would not be an overstatement to say that the recent, much-awaited 2008 corporate income tax reform is probably the most significant of all. Its significance rests primarily on its impact on foreign investors doing business in China.

New Corporate Income Tax Law

The Enterprise Income Tax Law of the People's Republic of China was passed by the Tenth National People's Congress on March 16, 2007, and went into effect on January 1, 2008. At the same time, the following measures were abolished: The People's Republic of China's Law of Foreign Invested Enterprises and Foreign Enterprises Income, which had been passed by the National People's Congress on April 9, 1991, and The Interim Regulations on Enterprise Income Tax of the People's Republic of China, which had been promulgated by the State Council on December 13, 1993. This means that both domestic enterprises and foreign invested enterprises can now enjoy the same taxation treatment under what is now known as the Unified Enterprises Income Tax Law.

Background of the New Legislation

In order to appreciate the new income tax law, it is necessary to understand the background leading to the birth of this legislation.

The Formation of the Two-Track Tax System Before the Reform and Its Defects

As China opens its doors to the world and to foreign investors, it has realized that it needs to continuously link up with international practices (与国际接轨). Therefore it began moving toward the unification of domestic enterprise taxes and foreign-invested enterprise taxes in the 1990s. Originally in the early 1990s, the Interim Regulations on Enterprise Income Tax of the People's Republic of China applied to domestic enterprises, while the People's Republic of China's Law of Foreign Invested Enterprises and Foreign Enterprises Income Tax applied to foreign companies. Thus, a two-track, parallel tax system was formed. The rate for domestic enterprises and foreign enterprises was 33 percent (inclusive of 30 percent state tax and 3 percent local tax). Since the opening up of the economy, for the purpose of attracting foreign capital, a great number of tax incentives have been offered to foreign invested enterprises, which include "the two-year tax exemption and three-year half-tax" policy for foreign invested manufacturing enterprises with operation periods exceeding 10 years. Some companies that are established in Special Economic Zones and Economic Technology Parks are able to enjoy even lower tax rates of 15 percent and 24 percent. Thus, foreign enterprises are able to enjoy preferential treatment in China.

Some domestic enterprises obtain identities as "foreign invested enterprises" either by setting up virtual joint ventures, or by establishing corporations outside China to reinvest back into China so that they can enjoy these tax incentives. Other foreign enterprises change their business address for consecutive enjoyment of the "the two-year tax exemption and three-year half-tax" policy. However, such actions are departures from the original purposes of these incentive policies.

The Formation of the Unified Tax System

The reform of the enterprise income tax law has required the consideration of many factors and their impact. Therefore, reforming the tax system has taken a longer time to evolve, while the economy is developing at high speed.

Internally, governments at different levels have different opinions, especially relating to enterprises of varied industries. For example, manufacturing enterprises in Special Economic Zones could enjoy "the two-year tax exemption and three-year half-tax" upon approval; in addition to a low tax rate of 15 percent before the 2008 tax reform. Now that such incentive policies have been abolished by the unification of taxes, the local governments of these Special Economic Zones have begun to worry about the loss of tax revenue caused by potential withdrawal of foreign capital and investments.

Externally, the 1997 Southeast Asia financing crisis forced many Southeast Asian countries to promote preferential conditions for foreign investors. China began to worry that corporate income tax reforms might cause capital withdrawals from China, and that these withdrawals would become inflows to the aforementioned countries. After becoming a member of the WTO, China was determined to promote the process of tax unification following the principles (such as fairness) of the WTO.

Due to these driving forces, in the last five years, the call for a unified system has gained greater support. Domestic companies had already been calling for years for fairness in treatment between domestic companies and foreign companies. The new legislation would also dish out tax incentives based upon industries, and relieve the pressure built upon the old incentives.

The Values of the New Law

The new income tax law has the following values:

- It has set the ground for fairer competition between domestic and foreign invested enterprises.
- It has established a taxation system with the legal representative of a company as the standard taxpaying unit or body.
- It has established a globally competitive tax rate system.
- It has established an industry-led tax incentive system that can be widely applicable.
- It has established a systematic and standardized anti–tax avoidance system.

The Framework of the New Law

The remainder of this chapter will discuss the key aspects of the 2008 China Corporate Income Tax Law in greater detail.

The Basic Framework of the New Legislation

There are 60 articles falling under 8 chapters in the Enterprise Income Tax Law. The basic framework consists of the following:

- *Chapter One—General Principles:* The unified definitions of taxpayers and rates; the differentiated definitions of resident enterprises, nonresident enterprises, and their tax liabilities;
- *Chapter Two—Taxable Income:* Definitions of income, deductions, and the establishment of the tax treatment of assets, including the computation of taxable income;
- *Chapter Three—Income Tax Payable:* Determination of tax credits and computation of income tax payable;
- *Chapter Four—Tax Incentives:* Structured primarily, according to the preferential treatment for industries and secondarily according to preferential treatment for regions;
- *Chapter Five—Withholding Tax at Source:* Determination of items and procedures of withholding tax at source;
- *Chapter Six—Special Tax Adjustments:* Standardization of transfer pricing; the establishment of the principles of a controlled company; prevention of thin capitalization and the establishment of special tax adjustments with accrued interest;
- *Chapter Seven—Tax Administration;*
- *Chapter Eight—Supplementary Provisions.*

The provisions stipulated in the 2008 Law of Enterprise Income Tax are quite general, and the Implementation Rules of the Law of Enterprise Income Tax were later issued on December 13, 2007. The Implementation Rules clarified the laws, and explained how the various regulations would be implemented. For instance, Clause 3 of Article 2 mentions the words "institutions and establishments," but there are no specifications for "institutions and establishments" given therein. In Article 4 of The Implementation Rules, the aforesaid "institution and establishments" is clearly defined.

As the complementary document of the Law of Enterprise Income Tax, the Implementation Rules are structured based on the same framework of the Law, and are also in accordance with the Law with respect to the usage of words and the arrangement of clauses. As such, the Implementation Rules enhance the operation of the Law of Enterprise Income Tax. In addition to the Law and the Implementation Rules, the Tax Authority at the state level continues to issue circulars to answer the public's questions about other aspects of the law.

The Important Points of the New Law

The following are some of the key points of the 2008 Corporate Income Tax Reform:

- The 2008 Law of Enterprise Income Tax has changed the previous method of differentiating taxpayer identity, which was based upon the source of capital for the enterprise: for instance, whether it was a foreign capital funded entity (that is, a Foreign Invested Enterprise), or a domestic capital funded entity. Instead, the new law stipulates that, except for sole proprietor enterprises and partnerships, all the enterprises and other profit-making organizations within the territory of China shall pay taxes in accordance with the law.
- Taking into consideration the tax burden of companies, the tax rates of neighboring countries, China's fiscal capabilities, and the sustainability of domestic and foreign invested enterprises, the Law has unified the tax rate at 25 percent. The development of tax rates for domestic and foreign investment enterprises are shown in Table 6.1.
- Development of tax rates.
- The new law also differentiates resident enterprises and nonresident enterprises. Their respective tax liabilities are also determined accordingly, and specified in the new legislation. Similar to the Individual Income Tax (IIT) law, the Enterprise Income Tax Law introduced the concepts of resident enterprises and nonresident enterprises. China adopted dual judgment criteria, based upon the registration location and the actual management location when differentiating between resident enterprises and

Table 6.1 Tax Rates and Tax Burdens

Enterprises		Tax Rate		Tax Burden
		Before Reform	After Reform	
Domestic Enterprises		33%	25%	Lowered
Foreign Invested Enterprises	Enterprises that did not enjoy tax incentives	33% (note)	25%	Lowered
	Enterprises that enjoyed tax incentives	15%/24%	25%	Raised

Note: The 33 percent rate is inclusive of 3 percent local tax.

nonresident enterprises. Compliance with either of these requirements will render the enterprise a resident of China.

- *Definition of resident enterprises:* The term *resident enterprises* refers
  to enterprises that are set up in China in accordance with the law,
  or that are set up in accordance with the laws of the foreign country (region) whose actual administration institutions are in China.
- *Definition of nonresident enterprises:* The term *nonresident enterprises*
  refers to enterprises that are set up in accordance with the laws of
  the foreign country (region), whose actual administration institutions are outside China, but have set up institutions or establishments in China, or have income originating from China without
  setting up institutions or establishments in China.
- *Definition of actual administration institution:* The term refers to the
  institution that implements actual overall administration and control over the enterprise's production operations, personnel management, finance, and property. However, this is a general
  definition, and the Tax Authority will make judgments based on
  specific situations. Subsequent decisions and judgments in later
  cases will eventually create precedents for standard practices. This
  is a key point that foreign enterprises should take into consideration when they plan to set up institutions in China.
- *Definition of institutions and establishments:* The term refers to
  institutions and establishments that conduct production and operations within China's territory. Where a nonresident enterprise
  authorizes an operating agency to conduct production and operations, including the signing of contracts on behalf of the commis-
  sioning units or individuals, or the depositing of money, and the

transferring of goods, the agency will be regarded as an institution and establishment that is set up by the nonresident enterprise within China.

The tax liabilities of resident enterprises and nonresident enterprises are detailed in Table 6.2.

The Accrual Accounting System

Income Tax Payable

One key development of the 2008 Corporate Income Tax Law is the adoption of the Accrual Basis of Accounting/Accrual System for purposes of ensuring the matching of taxable income and deducted expenses before tax. This new development is aligned with international tax practice.

The following are some examples:

- Income from equity investments such as dividends and bonus: income will be recognized based on the profit distribution date determined by the investor, as opposed to actual cash payment point as previously;
- Interest income will be recognized on the date when the debtor's interest is due, based on the loan agreement;
- Rental income will be recognized on the date when tenant rent is due, based on the rental contract agreement;
- Computation of taxable incomes.

The computing formula is specified in the Law as follows:

$$\text{Taxable income} = \text{income} - \text{deduction}$$

- Income includes income from sale of goods, income from labor services, equity investments such as dividends and bonuses, interest income, rental income, income from royalties, income from donations, and other incomes.
- Deductions include costs, fees, taxes, losses, and other expenses.

Deductible Items

A few key points relating to the deductible items need specific attention:

Table 6.2 Tax Liabilities of Resident and Nonresident Enterprises

Type of taxpayers / Applicable Rate	Income Originating in China	Income Originating Outside China	
		With actual relations to institutions and establishments in China	Without actual relations to institutions and establishments in China
Resident enterprises	25%	25%	25%
Nonresident enterprises — With institutions and establishments in China	25%	25%	Tax Exempted
Nonresident enterprises — Without any institutions or establishments in China but have income originating in China	10%	N/A	Tax Exempted

- Deductible expenses include reasonable salary expenses incurred by the enterprise, although there is no specification of what constitutes a "reasonable salary."
- With respect to welfare expenses for the employees, workers' union funds, and training fees for employees, the portions that do not exceed 14 percent, 2 percent, 2.5 percent of these expenses respectively are allowable deductions. The Law still (as before) specifies percentages on such expenses to limit their deductibility against income.
- Interest expenses originating from loans are deductible.
- Entertainment expenses incurred in relation to production and operation activities will be taxed on a basis of 60 percent of the incurred amount. But it shall not exceed 0.5 percent of the revenue of the year.
- Approved advertising and business promotion expenses that do not exceed 15 percent of the revenue of the year are deductible. The excess can be carried over for deduction in following tax years.
- Special funds that are withdrawn for environmental protection and ecology recoveries in accordance with the associated regulations (no deduction is permitted if the purpose for the withdrawal of funds is changed) are deductible.
- Insurance fees paid in accordance with the associated regulations of property insurance are deductible.
- If a nonresident enterprise establishes a permanent establishment (PE) in China, and this nonresident enterprise's headquarters expenses are incurred in relation to the PE's operations, the expenses are deductible (with valid proof and supporting evidence).
- In relation to the expenses from charitable donations incurred by enterprises, the portion within 12 percent of the total annual profit may be deducted from the taxable income.

The following expenses cannot be deducted:

- The business insurance paid for investors or employees by the enterprise (except for special items).
- Administration and management fees paid among the enterprises, rentals, and royalties within the internal operating institutions of

the enterprise, and interest paid among internal operating institutions of nonfinancial enterprises.

In addition to the above provisions, the enterprises' deficits for the tax year can be carried forward, and are set off using the future income in the following years. However, such carry-forwards and set-offs can only be performed within a limited period of five years.

Computation of Income Tax Payable

The formula is as follows:

$$\text{Income tax payable} = \text{taxable income} \times \text{applicable rate} - \text{tax deducted} - \text{tax offset}$$

Tax offset includes direct and indirect ones:

- Direct tax offset.
- Where income from equity investments, such as dividends and bonuses originating from outside the territory of China, is earned by a foreign enterprise directly or indirectly controlled by a China resident enterprise, the portion of tax (that is, actual income tax paid outside the territory by the foreign enterprise) pro-rated to the latter may be used for offset by such a resident enterprise.
- The term *direct or indirect control* refers to situations where the resident enterprise holds a portion of more than 20 percent of the foreign enterprise's equity.

Preferential Tax Treatment

As mentioned above, before the tax reform, China had various tax incentive policies for foreign enterprises that were established in special economic zones, coastal economic zones, and technology parks or zones. These are collectively termed "regional preferential treatment" (区域税务优惠). Such policies did attract foreign capital. However, many problems surfaced as they developed. For example, preferential tax treatment resulted in the fast development of many coastal cities, but at the same time, neglected the development of many inland rural areas. This has further aggravated the very severe inequality of wealth distribution in recent years. In the 2008 tax reform, the Chinese government has adjusted the preferential tax treatment to one that is industry-focused rather than regionally focused: that is, preferential tax policies are granted to enterprises in specific industries, seconded by regional emphasis; rather than according to pure "regional focus" (see Table 6.3).

Transitional Arrangements for Tax Rates

Given that many foreign companies, especially manufacturing companies, had been enjoying lower tax rates previously, the Chinese government has come up with transitional arrangements on tax rates to buffer the tax burdens of many such foreign companies. They serve to relieve such impact on foreign enterprises.

From January 1, 2008, the low tax rate of 15 percent, which most of the enterprises enjoyed before, will be gradually raised to the statutory rate of 25 percent from 2008 to 2012, namely: 18 percent in 2008, 20 percent in 2009, 22 percent in 2010, 24 percent in 2011, and 25 percent in 2012. The enterprises that paid taxes at a 24 percent rate before will pay a rate of 25 percent from 2008 onwards.

Withholding Tax

The payable income tax from income obtained by nonresident enterprises is subject to taxes withheld at the source, with the payer as the withholding agent. The tax payment is withheld from the amount paid, or the payable amount due from each tax payment and payable amount of the withholding agent. Before the tax reform, dividends paid to overseas parent companies by foreign enterprises were exempted from withholding tax. After the reform, the rate of withholding tax for dividends, bonuses, interest, royalties, and capital gains had been reduced to 10 percent (the law originally provided for 20 percent; now it is implemented at 10 percent). Some of the withholding taxes can be lowered if the parent companies are from countries that have entered into double tax treaty agreements with China.

Special Tax Adjustments in the New Law

Special Tax Adjustments are mainly involved in the following areas:

- Standardization of transfer pricing
- Rules of controlled foreign companies

Table 6.3 New Preferential Tax Policies

Types of Preferential Policies	Items	Policy
	Income from interest of government bonds	Tax Exempted
	Equity investments such as dividends and bonuses from qualified resident enterprises[1]	Tax Exempted
	Income from equity investments such as dividends and bonuses obtained from resident enterprises by nonresident enterprises that have set up institutions or establishments in China, with an actual relationship with such institutions or establishments[2]	Tax Exempted
	Income of qualified nonprofit organizations	Tax Exempted
Preferential Treatment Granted on Types of Incomes or Expenses	Qualified expenses for research and development	Additional 50% deduction or amortization
	The wages paid by enterprises for job placements for the disabled and other placements encouraged by the state	Additional 100% deduction
	Venture investment enterprises that engage in venture investment encouraged by the state[3]	Deduction amount of 70% of investments
	Qualified fixed assets	Accelerated depreciation
	Income obtained by enterprises from the production of products in line with state industrial policies through the comprehensive use of resources	Discount on revenue amount

Table 6.3 (*Continued*)

Preferential Tax Rate	Small-scale enterprises with minimal profits that are qualified[4]	15%
	High and new technology enterprises supported by the state[5]	15%
	Income from engaging in projects of agriculture, forestry, animal husbandry, and fisheries	Tax Exempted or Lower Taxable Amount
	Income from investment and operation of infrastructure projects with key state support	Two-Year Tax Holiday and Three-Year Half-Tax[6]
	Income from engaging in qualified projects of environmental protection, energy, and water conservation	Two-Year Tax Holiday and Three-Year Half-Tax[6]
Preferential Treatment on Taxable Amount	Income of high and new technology enterprises that are registered in the Special Economic Zones (including Shenzhen, Zhuhai, Shantou, Xiamen, and Hainan) and the Shanghai Pudong New Area after January 1, 2008 (inclusive of the same day) with support from the state	Two-Year Tax Holiday and Three-Year Half-Tax[6]
	Income from qualified transfer of techniques[7]	Tax Exempted or Lower Taxable Amount
	Enterprise income tax shared by the local government of the ethnic autonomous locality	Tax Exempted or Lower Taxable Amount

[1]Refers to investment interests derived from resident enterprises' direct investments in other resident enterprises. Investment interest from consistent holdings of stocks that are publicly issued, and listed by resident enterprises for less than 12 months are not included.

[2]Investment interest from consistent holdings of stocks that are publicly issued, and listed by resident enterprises for less than 12 months are not included.

(*Continued*)

Table 6.3 (*Continued*)

[3]For venture enterprises that have invested in unlisted small-to-medium new technology enterprises by means of equity investment for more than two years, 70 percent of the investment amount in such enterprises may be deducted against the taxable income of the venture capital enterprise for the year in which the two-year holding is completed. When the amount of the deduction is not fully utilized in that year, the unused amount is allowed to be carried forward to the following tax years.

[4]For industrial enterprises, the annual taxable income should not exceed RMB 300,000. The number of staff should not exceed 100, and the total assets should not exceed RMB 30,000,000. For other enterprises, the annual taxable income should not exceed RMB 300,000. The number of staff should not exceed 80, and the total assets should not exceed RMB 10,000,000.

[5]The term *state-encouraged new technology enterprises* refers to enterprises having independent ownership of core intellectual property, which simultaneously meet the following criteria:

The products (services) fall within the "Scope of State-encouraged New Technologies";

The ratio of research and development expenditure to the enterprise's sales shall not be less than the ratio stipulated;

The ratio of sales (or service) income from new technology products to total revenue shall not be less than the ratio stipulated;

The percentage of employees working in science and technology field shall not be less than the ratio stipulated;

Other conditions may be stipulated by the verification and administrative measures over new technology enterprises.

[6]It will start from the tax year when revenue is achieved from production and operation.

[7]During the first tax year, the portion of technology transfer belonging to resident enterprises that is not more than RMB 5,000,000 is tax exempted. The portion that exceeds RMB 5,000,000 will enjoy tax rates equal to half the original tax rate imposed.

Table 6.4 Withholding Tax Rate of Countries That Have Entered into Double Tax Treaty Agreements with China

Type	Mauritius	USA	Hong Kong	Singapore
Dividends and bonus	5%	10%	5% ($\geq$25%) 10% (<25%)	5% ($\geq$25%) 10% (<25%)
Interest	10%	10%	7%	7% (financial institutions) 10% (others)
Royalty	10%	10%	7%	10%

Note: Applicable to income transfer from domestic enterprises to overseas enterprises. The percentages in brackets above indicate the equity investment of the Hong Kong and Singapore parent companies in their subsidiaries.

- Prevention of thin capitalization
- Standardization of transfer pricing
- Arm's length principle

Business transactions between enterprises and their affiliated parties should observe the arm's length principle. Otherwise, the tax authority will have the power to make adjustments by measures, based on comparable noncontrolled prices, resale pricing, cost plus, net profit of transaction, profit division, and other measures to apply the transfer price, in order to ensure that enterprises observe the arm's length principle.

In practice, many affiliates actually transfer profits by means of "buying at high prices and selling at low prices", or the reverse. Given the new law, which effectively spells out transfer pricing as a target, the enterprises will have to think twice before proceeding with such practices. The Tax Authority may require adjustments in respect of the use of those methods.

Cost-Sharing Agreement

Affiliates that conduct joint development and intangible property transfer, or jointly provide or accept the cost of services can share costs according to the arm's length principle

This means that, when a Chinese enterprise conducts joint development and intangible property transfers, or jointly provides or accepts the cost of services, and pays the costs to an overseas affiliate as agreed in the Cost-sharing Agreement (in practice, this needs to be approved by the Tax Authority), the payment should not be recognized as royalty fees or service fees. The company will not be required to withhold taxes when making such payments to overseas affiliates.

Advance Pricing Arrangement

Through consultation and confirmation between the Tax Authority and the enterprise, advance pricing arrangements can be made that confirm the enterprise's pricing principles and computational methods for transactions among the enterprise's affiliates.

Liability of Providing Materials

Enterprises and affiliates, and enterprises that have similarities with the investigated enterprise (in respect to business scope and operations) are required to provide materials and information related to the transactions when called upon.

Rules of Controlled Foreign Companies

Resident enterprises or enterprises controlled by resident enterprises or residents who establish companies in countries (regions) where the actual tax rate is below 12.5 percent, and where part of the profits of such companies are not allocated to the resident enterprises due to unreasonable business operations, will have to reallocate such profits back to the resident enterprise; according to the Tax Authority in the tax year concerned. The Tax Authority has the power to make any adjustments by reasonable methods, if necessary.

What Does *Controlled* Mean?

The term refers to a resident enterprise or an individual resident of China directly or indirectly holding 10 percent or more of total voting shares, and where such resident enterprise(s) and individual resident(s) jointly hold more than 50 percent of total shares of the foreign enterprise; where the shareholding percentage of resident enterprise(s) and individual resident(s) of China do not meet the percentage standard as stipulated, but substantial control is formed over the foreign enterprise with regards to shareholding, financing, business, purchase and sales, and so forth.

Under such stipulations, some Chinese resident enterprises that reduce their total global tax burden through tax havens have to make new arrangements.

Preventing Thin Capitalization

Due to the difference between the taxation of debt financing and equity financing (interest expenses can be deducted before tax, while dividend expenses cannot be deducted and will be double-taxed for corporate tax and withholding tax), multinational companies will try to avoid tax by increasing debt financing and reducing equity financing.

The new Law of Corporate Income Tax stipulates that the interest expenses resulting from the overincurring of debt investment (to equity investment) that the enterprise accepts from its affiliates shall not be deducted when computing taxable income. The Implementation Rules have made explanations for debt investment as well as equity investment, while the practices will be further stipulated by financial and tax authorities of the State Council.

In the 2008 Law, besides being empowered to make special tax adjustments, the Tax Authority is also empowered to impose interest on late payments. For example, if upon reassessment by the Tax Authority that there is underpaid tax, an additional 5 percent over and above the banks' interest rate will be imposed on the amount of underpayment. If the company is able to provide supporting documents and proof of expediency in settlement, the additional 5 percent will be waived. However, the punitive interest cannot be deducted when computing taxable income.

Where transactions between an enterprise and its related parties do not comply with the arm's length principle, or an enterprise makes other arrangements without bona fide commercial purposes, the Tax Authority has the right to make tax adjustments within 10 years from the tax year when the transactions occurred.

Conclusion

With the new tax Reform of 2008, foreign companies will have to be more vigilant in planning their tax road map when doing business in

China. The Chinese Tax Authorities will continue to release new circulars to clarify situations encountered by companies in practice. As much as the new Tax Reform offers challenges to foreign businesses, it has also offered greater clarity, regularized practices, and stepped up enforcement efforts. The 2008 Tax Reform is a major step forward in China's tax and economic development.

7

Audit and Annual Inspection

L ike business people throughout the world, investors who do businesses and set up companies in China will be required to perform
audits on their companies. Internationally, all CFOs understand that
auditing is a statutory requirement. The audit calls for the auditor to
express an opinion about the truth and fairness of the company's financial statements. This requirement is almost universal throughout the
world, and it is no different in China. However, in China, there are
certain audit and audit-related peculiarities that we will discuss in this
chapter to guide CFOs on how to handle audit requirements of their
subsidiaries in China.

Audit of Financial Statements Under the PRC GAAP

Many countries throughout the world today are harmonizing toward
the International Financial Reporting Standards (IFRS), and China
is also moving in this direction. However, at this point of time, the
Chinese PRC Generally Accepted Accounting Principles ("GAAP")
are still the recognized standards. The Chinese government adopted
the new PRC Accounting Standards at the beginning of 2007. They
require all publicly listed companies in China to prepare financial statements in accordance with 39 accounting standards.

This requirement extends to all foreign invested enterprises, including Wholly Foreign Owned Enterprises (WFOEs), Joint Ventures (JVs), and Representative Offices (ROs). The auditor is responsible for expressing an opinion about the truth and fairness of the financial statement. Similar to the laws in many countries, notwithstanding the responsibility of the auditors, the legal representatives of the enterprises and the chief representatives of the representative offices must also take full responsibility for the truthfulness, compliance, and completeness of these financial statements.

The single most significant issue of the annual audit is that the audit opinions and the audit financial statements form a basis for ascertaining the income tax and distributable profits of the company.

Annual Tax Assessment

In the 2008 Corporate Income Tax Act (see Chapter 6), Chinese authorities recognize the difference between taxable income and accounting income. Accounting income must be verified by the auditor. It forms the basis by which tax authorities make adjustments to arrive at the taxable income. This process is known as Annual Tax Assessment (年度税务汇算清缴).

The annual tax assessment is seen by most foreign companies, in almost all contexts, to be something even more important than the audit itself, because it concerns the taxes that the companies have to pay.

Extended Corporate Compliance and Regulatory Requirements

In addition to the audit and taxation requirements, under Chinese company laws and regulations, there are various extended corporate compliance and regulatory requirements. The CFO may understand these as extensions and "required derivatives" of the audit.

Foreign Exchange Audit

One of the key requirements for Foreign Investment Enterprises (FIEs) operating in China is the Foreign Exchange Audit. Traditionally and up to the current point in time, this is probably the single most important difference between FIEs and domestic companies operating in China. By virtue of being an FIE, a company is allowed to establish a foreign exchange bank account. Domestic Chinese companies largely do business in China in RMB, and therefore may not be given the approval to open foreign exchange accounts (see Chapter 4).

But the capability to utilise foreign-currency bank accounts brings with it greater regulations by the China government. Therefore, at the end of the year, whenever the auditor carries out the annual statutory audit on the financial statements, there is also a requirement to carry out a Foreign Currency Audit (外汇审计) on the foreign exchange bank account. The auditor is required to audit and review the foreign currency transactions that have occurred during the year via the foreign currency bank account. The auditor is also required to opine on whether the company has conducted foreign currency transactions in accordance with Chinese rules and regulations, especially the regulations of the State Administration of Foreign Exchange (SAFE). In recent years, SAFE has been more stringent in the enforcement of foreign exchange controls and regulations. This has inevitably put greater pressures on companies and the auditors.

Annual Inspection

One of the other most significant differences between China and other countries is the Annual Inspection (年检). In China, the completion of the audit is not the end of the process. In addition to the auditor's opinion on the financial statements, the company is also responsible to ensure that these results are submitted to various government authorities.

The administrative processes of annual inspection in China require companies to complete standard forms (including the audited financial statements and auditor's report) for the "original approving authorities" and agencies. The original approving authorities are the ones that issued the licenses and certificates when the company was incorporated. These original departments will accordingly "inspect" to see whether the company has complied with relevant laws and regulations during the year. Each government agency or department will inspect and review the submitted information, and the audit results that are relevant to its own department. For example, we have mentioned that the SAFE will inspect foreign currency transactions. Similarly, the State Administration of Industry and Commerce (SAIC) will inspect to see whether the company has conducted business during the year according to its business scope.

In recent years, in the main Tier One cities in China, such as Shanghai, in order to help companies and to facilitate the annual inspection process, all the government agencies practice what is known as the United Annual Inspection (联合年检). Under this system, all the government agencies and officers will gather at one place to receive submissions and carry out inspections. Previously, before the United Annual Inspection was in place, the companies actually needed to submit audit results and annual inspection information from one agency to another. Today, we see greater use of computerization in annual submissions. However, hard-paper submission is still required.

In most cities, the Annual Inspection for the year ending on December 31 must be completed by the end of April of the following year. (see "Audit Deadline" below. For these reasons, companies often outsource the Annual Inspection to expert consultants.)

The company's CFO must bear in mind that although the auditor may issue a clean opinion on the audited financial statements, this is not the completion of the entire process. The company also needs to ensure that it passes the Annual Inspection by the government departments. If not, there is a possibility that licenses or certificates will not be renewed, and the company may not be able to carry on its business operations.

Audit Deadlines

Audit timing affects great numbers of business people. These include the accountants, the directors and the company staff, the auditors, and the government agencies. In addition, all companies in China have the same accounting year-end, December 31 of each year. Government authorities do not allow any other accounting year-end. This is very different from practices in other countries. Given the regulations and requirements on timing, there is tremendous pressure on resources, because so many resources are tied up to meet various integrated objectives at one point in time. From the end of December every year through the end of April the following year, many people find it very difficult to carry out their company business as normal. The entire situation is further aggravated by the fact that there are so many companies in China.

As soon as the year ends in December, companies must have their accounts audited in January or February—April at the latest. Regulations require that after the audit, companies must clear annual inspections by the end of April at the latest. There is only a very slim possibility that a company can seek an extension from the authorities.

A CFO handling a China subsidiary must plan very carefully in view of the audit requirements, the extended regulatory requirements, and the timing constraints. These can be complicated by other requirements from parent companies. For example, requirements to present audited financial statements, in accordance with parent companies' accounting standards and timing requirements, resulting from the consolidation needs of holding companies.

Differences Between the Parent Company's Accounting Year-End and China's Accounting Standards

One of the biggest challenges in the audit is the differences in accounting and auditing standards. Foreign investors coming from all over the world to do business in China have to reckon with the different China accounting standards. The accounting standards in China are very much geared towards tax, foreign currency controls, and administration procedures. Therefore, foreign investors have to understand that accounting standards in China can somewhat be different from those of their home countries.

Many of the foreign CFOs who come to China are accustomed to international auditing requirements. However, many of these international auditing practices are not practiced by China auditors. For example, normally when the head office issues instructions for the China subsidiaries to carry out an audit, there is naturally a head office financial consolidation package and head office auditor's instructions that need to be submitted by the subsidiaries to the head office. When these are being explained to a Chinese auditor, he may be quite unfamiliar with them which can be compounded by language problems. So, the head office auditor may find it very difficult to ask the subsidiary's local Chinese auditor to perform certain audit practices and procedures that are very common in Western countries: for example, the circularization of accounts receivables to confirm amounts owed by customers.

Standard Procedure

A firm had purchased certain software programs and categorized them as intangible assets. In the first year, the client sought agreement from the tax authorities to recompute amortization of the intangible assets over five years. In the second year, at the year-end closing, the tax authorities instructed the client to amortize the intangibles over 10 years instead of the original five years. The consequence was that this actually increased the company's profit, leading to a higher income tax. However, the firm did not contest the request of the tax authorities and instead had to prolong the useful life of the intangibles leading to the increase in profit.

Given the above situation, and as more and more foreign investors come to China, it has become the intention of the Chinese government to harmonize China's accounting and auditing standards to those of the rest of the world. This is to allow foreign investors to understand the Chinese accounting and business environment better. It should also bring China closer to the international practices.

Many small local Chinese auditors may not practice circularization of debtors. Today, many international auditors' practices in China would have to circularize debtors to the closest scrutiny, so that they can ensure that debtors understand very specifically what it means when they put a stamp on a debtor's circularization. As another example, stock-take observations for many small Chinese audits are not practiced. However, in the last 10 years or so, as foreign auditors began to share their international audit procedures and practices, many of the small local Chinese audit firms face much competition, and are now pressured to adopt international audit procedures. The overall climate will see a tremendous shift of local audit practices and procedures toward international standards. This works to the advantage of foreign investors doing business in China.

Besides the difference in accounting standards and auditing procedures, the differences in the accounting year-end can be significant. This is especially so if the subsidiary in China is a major component of the entire parent group. The Chinese subsidiary is mandated to have a fixed year-end at December 31, while the parent company can have a different year-end. Thus, for purposes of consolidation at the parent company level, the CFO may require the China subsidiary's auditor to audit adjustments, and reconcile the accounts according to the parent company's 12-month period. This effort also requires additional audit procedures and work for the auditor.

The Audit Industry in China

A CFO must understand the audit industry in China in order to select a good auditor. The audit industry in China consists of three main types of firms:

- The Big Four firms
- Mid-tier international firms
- Local Chinese audit firms

The Big Four audit firms entered China as early as the beginning of its economic reforms some 30 years ago. They have brought with them international audit methodologies, audit practices, and procedures that were traditionally less common in China. Most international CFOs will be very familiar with the risk-based audit approaches adopted by the Big Four firms, and the other international firms also have good international audit training programs that are adapted to Chinese standards. During the last 20 years or so, the Big Four firms and the mid-tier international firms have, in fact, trained a tremendous number of Chinese auditors. Most multinational and Fortune 500 companies coming to do business in China will almost inevitably prefer to use the Big Four audit firms that the parent company is currently using. Due to the various reasons mentioned above, as well as the rich diversity of the Chinese business environment, the Big Four firms usually command a price premium over many other audit firms in China.

In the last 10 to 15 years, the mid-tier international firms have also been making their entry into China. Like the Big Four audit firms, the mid-tier firms have also been introducing international audit methodologies and risk-based audit approaches. A majority of the mid-tier international audit firms have collaborations with the bigger local China audit firms. Through such collaborations, the mid-tier international firms are able to bring know-how and international audit practices to local China firms. Thereby they, raise the standards of the local China firms in terms of quality of work, audit methodologies, and audit procedures. The values and know-how that the mid-tier international firms are bringing into China also allow them to command a price premium over the local Chinese audit firms. The mid-tier international firms have also been training and developing a large number of international accountants in China to meet the demands of the industry. This has become one of the largest and fastest growing segment in the market.

The last category of audit firms includes the small local audit firms. Their practices are very form-based and include a less risk-based approach (which international CFOs will understand). Many of the local Chinese auditors' audit methodologies and procedures are carried out with an emphasis on complying only with statutory year-end compliance requirements: that is, the annual inspection requirements of the Chinese government. The small local Chinese audit procedures are very substantive and less risk-based. It is, therefore, not surprising to find that local Chinese audit firms only meet demands of companies who see statutory compliance as their principal requirement. The small local Chinese CPA fees are therefore low, and the audits are carried out over a very short period of time. These firms also deploy relatively few resources.

Trends in the Usage of Audit Firms

Multinational companies, big conglomerates in China, and state-owned enterprises find themselves using the Big Four audit firms and the mid-tier international firms most frequently. This happens especially when companies are going public in the overseas international and capital markets. This has also raised the requirements in terms of quality, service, and pricing of international audit firms operating in China. It has also created demand by larger foreign companies in China to use international audit firms, and adopt international audit practices. Given this development, the audit industry in China will enter a phase of consolidation. Typically, the smaller audit firms will need to link up with international audit firms and adopt international practices. If they do not do so, they may be left out because their clients will go elsewhere. These clients will come not only from foreign companies, but also from local companies going global. Paramount among these developments is a greater demand for service quality from clients, whether from international companies operating in China, or from local companies operating in China. There is greater demand in terms of the speed of delivery of service, deadlines, and resource constraints. Many companies, especially the small and midsize companies, find that they either have to pay a premium for good-quality service, or they will be reduced to using a firm that is of poor quality. But there is still time for the market to consolidate and find its equilibrium. The CFO doing business in China has to find the right audit firm to serve his or her company.

Expectations of Auditors

Earlier in this chapter we discussed the requirements for auditors in China. One of the most important issues is what a foreign company and a CFO should expect of an auditor in China.

The common expectation is fairly unique to China. Many look upon the auditor as their primary assistant to start business in China, not just someone who audits financial statements. CFOs very much expect auditors to be more like consultants. Taking on a consultant's role will imply that the auditor has to be well-versed in information areas related to company structure, regulations, employment, and other areas besides auditing and accounting. At the same time, local Chinese auditors need to begin to understand the demands of foreign companies. The mid-tier audit firms and the Big Four audit firms also need to understand other aspects of doing business in China. They should be able to satisfy the needs of ever-demanding CFOs for business advisors, and to provide solutions for the different problems that a company may encounter. The role and function of the auditor is somewhat blurred. There is also a natural conflict of interest if auditors are not careful to maintain their independent role. In this respect, many mid-tier international audit firms are competing with consulting affiliates to create solutions for their clients.

Conclusion

We have discussed extensively the foreign companies in China, the governance of these companies, the auditing industry in China, as well as the expectations of CFOs. We believe that the auditing industry will continue to evolve as the economic reforms in China continue for the next 30 years. Many of the developments that are happening or have happened in the world outside China will probably be transported into China, and adapted at even greater speed. This should be able to help China develop its next phase of economic reform.

8

Hiring and Employment

A CFO who does business in China must understand hiring and employment practices. Financially, employment and hiring involve cost in many aspects. The most direct, of course, are the payroll costs. This is very much the business of the CFO, and not just of the human resources manager. However, many foreign companies doing business in China do not have a full-time manager to take care of human resource matters. The CFO, or the finance manager (like many companies in other countries) doubles or triples up as administration, HR, and IT head. This chapter introduces the key aspects of hiring and employment.

Hiring Procedures

The hunt for people normally starts even before the company is established. However, the official contractual relationship with an employee normally starts when the company acquires its business license.

Requirements in Hiring

In China, upon obtaining a business license, a company must establish the related Company Social Security Accounts. These Social Security Accounts include Pensions, Basic Medical Insurance, Unemployment

Insurance, Maternity Insurance, and Work-related Injury Insurance. (In addition, the company is required to register a Salary Handbook. See "Personnel File for Chinese Staff" later in this chapter.) The company also needs to sign the "protocol contract" with the related Personnel Files Maintenance Center to maintain the personnel files of local staff.

Chinese payroll regulations outline general procedures for hiring (or termination) of local or foreign employees.

The Written Labor Contract (LC) should be executed between the employee and employer on the new employee's first working day, for both locals and foreign employees. A Labor Contract should specify the following matters:

- The name, domicile, and legal representative or main person in charge of the employer company
- The name, domicile, and number of the resident ID card or other valid identity document of the employee
- The terms of the employment contract
- The job description and the place of work
- Working hours, rest, and leave
- Labor compensation
- Social insurance for Chinese staff
- Labor protection, working conditions, and protection against occupational hazards

In addition to the required terms mentioned above, an employer and an employee may agree to stipulate other matters in the employment contract, such as the probationary period, training, confidentiality, supplementary insurance and benefits, and so forth.

The employer can set the probationary period in the labor contract, which is based on the employment term or period. Under the law, however, six months is the maximum probationary period. A labor contract that is being renewed should not include a probationary period. The salary during the probationary period should not be less than 80 percent of the normal salary.

Personnel File for Chinese Staff

Every Chinese employee has a personnel file, which details important records and documents education, work experiences, political participation, criminal records (if any), and so forth. In the Chinese administrative system, such a personnel file dates back from elementary education and continues throughout the entire career. This system allows the government to monitor the movement of the individual according to employers.

Labor Handbook

The Labor Handbook (劳动手册) keeps records of working history. The employer needs to maintain the Handbook and stamp it (as proof of employment) for the period when the employee works for the company.

Chinese staff are classified by *hukou* (户口 or residency), which means a permanent residence in a city or town registered in the Public Security System. The requirements are different for an employee, whose *hukou* is not in the city where he or she works.

An employer needs to carry out the registration with the Labor Bureau within seven days after hiring a new employee. The required registration procedures include the following steps:

- Register the hiring information with the Labor Bureau
- Transfer the Personnel File to the Personnel Files Maintenance Center for the local staff whose *hukou* is the same as the Company location
- Transfer the new employee's Social Insurance and Housing Fund account into the Company's records.

Two issues need special attention:

- For those who have no Social Insurance account, such as recent graduates, the employer needs to register their information with the Social Insurance and Housing Fund Center, and set up the new employees' personnel accounts.
- There is a different Social Insurance for staff whose *hukou* is not the same as the company's location.

Hiring Foreign Staff

According to government regulations, any foreigner seeking employment in China must meet the following conditions:

- Between the ages of 18 and 60 for males, and between 18 and 55 for females
- In good health
- Possess professional skills and job experience required for the intended employment
- Possess no criminal record
- Have a clearly-defined employer
- Possess a valid passport, or other international travel document in lieu of the passport

In addition, the post to be filled by the foreign recruit must be:

- A post of special need
- A post that cannot be filled by any domestic candidates for the time being
- A post that violates no government work regulations

Foreign staff includes residents of Taiwan, Hong Kong, and Macau, since the regulations are quite similar to those for foreigners.

When a company decides to hire a foreigner, it needs to apply for an Employment Approval License, an Employment Permit, and a Residence Permit for the foreigner:

- The Employment Approval License must be applied for before the foreigner enters China.
- The Employment Permit is a certificate for the foreigner or expatriate working in China. It is a certificate registered with the Labor Bureau.
- The Residence Permit is a certificate for the expatriate staying in China. It is registered with the Entry and Exit Administration Bureau. It should be a multiple entry and exit visa.

The employer should apply with the Labor Bureau for the Employment License to get the initial approval for employing the foreign employee before his or her actual entry. Once the application is approved, the Employment License of the foreigner will be granted to the employer. Then, the employee must contact the authorized organizations (for instance, the Shanghai Municipality Foreign Trade) to apply for the Z visa (employment visa) notification letter. With the original Employment License and notification letter, the foreigner can then apply for the Z visa at the Chinese embassy or consulate in his own country. After the foreigner enters China with the Z visa, the employer should apply the Employment Permit and Residence Permit with the authorities.

For residents of Hong Kong and Macau, only the Employment Permit is required. But endorsement is also needed for Taiwan residents.

Monthly Payroll Processes

Upon hiring employees, the company needs to establish its payroll system properly. The system must comply with Chinese rules and regulations, as well as with the company's own policies and procedures. Here are the key general procedures for a payroll system in China.

Key Points in Payroll Calculations

For the local staff, the mandatory contributions are Social Insurance and the Housing Fund. The tax-exempt income amount was just recently increased to RMB 2000 per month from RMB 1600 per month, effective March 2008. The employer needs to withhold the Social Insurance, the Housing Fund, and individual income tax, and make payments every month to the relevant authorities. The employer is the legal withholding agent for these items.

Social Insurance normally includes five categories:

1. Pension
2. Basic Medical Insurance
3. Unemployment Insurance
4. Maternity Insurance
5. Work-related Injury Insurance

Social Insurance and the Housing Fund are to be paid by both employees and employers. Table 8.1 lists the rates of each category in Shanghai. The rates may differ in different cities, depending on the published official standard of living indices.

TABLE 8.1 Social Insurance Rates in Shanghai

Social Benefits	Employee	Employer
Pension[1]	8%	22%
Basic Medical Insurance[2]	2%	12%
Unemployment Insurance[3]	1%	2%
Maternity Insurance[4]	0%	0.5%
Work-related Injury Insurance[5]	0%	0.5%
Housing Fund[6]	7%	7%

[1]Announcement No. 45 in 2004, Shanghai Government Office. 沪府办发(2004) 45 号。No. 36 Announcement in 2003, Shanghai Pension Subcenter of Social Insurance Center. 沪劳保养发(2003) 36号。
[2]Order No. 92, Shanghai Municipal Government. 市政府令第 92号。Announcement No. 77 in 2000, Shanghai Medical Insurance Center. 沪医保发(2000) 77号.
[3]Announcement No. 7 in 1999, Shanghai Government Office. 沪府办发(1999) 7号。Announcement No. 1 in 2001, Shanghai Pension Sub-Center of Social Insurance Center. 沪劳保养发(2001) 1号。
[4]Order No. 33 in 2004, Shanghai Municipal Government. 市政府令(2004) 第33号。
[5]Order No. 29 in 2004, Shanghai Municipal Government. 市政府令(2004) 第29号。
[6]No. 42 Announcement in 1999, Shanghai Housing Fund Center. 沪公积金发(1999) 42号。

Please note that each year, usually in April and July, the city government will revise the Social Insurance and Housing Fund bases, and adjust the maximum and minimum applicable salary cap.

For foreigners, the tax exempt amount is RMB 4,800 per month.[1] There is no Social Insurance compliance requirement currently.

Overtime Payments and Holidays

The following are some key regulations relating to overtime and public holidays. The employing unit shall, according to the following standards, pay laborers remunerations higher than those for normal working hours under any of the following circumstances:

1. 150 percent of the normal wages if the extension of working hours is arranged.
2. 200 percent of the normal wages if the extended hours are arranged on days of rest, and no deferred rest can be taken.
3. 300 percent of the normal wages if the extended hours are arranged on statutory holidays, or unused paid annual vacations.

TABLE 8.2   Public Holidays

Holiday[1]	Number of Days
New Year Day	1 day
Spring Festival	3 days
Qing Ming Day	1 day (Ancestor's Prayer Day)
May Day (Labor Day)	1 day
Dumpling Festival	1 day
Mid-Autumn Festival	1 day
National Day	3 days

[1]Arrangement of National Annual Leaves and Memorial Days. December 14, 2007. State Council of P. R. China. 全国年节及纪念日放假办法 2007年12月14日国务院。

At the beginning of 2008, the Chinese government announced two regulations relating to arrangements for public holidays and for paid annual vacation of employees (see Tables 8.2 and 8.3).

Public holidays and weekends are not included as paid annual vacations. It is important to take note that very frequently, public holidays are strung along to create a longer stretch of holidays. For instance, if a public holiday falls on Monday, Tuesday, or Wednesday, the government may publish guidance for companies to work on the Saturday and Sunday before the holiday, and not work on the subsequent Thursday and Friday. The whole week will then be a holiday week. This is the well-known "golden week." In 2008, with the announcement of the new public holidays, there is an effort by the government to spread out the public holidays, and lessen the number of golden weeks.

Minimum Salary

Salary, excluding mandatory Social Insurance, Housing Fund, and Overtime payments, should be no less than the minimum salary, as stipulated by law. The minimum salary is determined by each specific province or area's regulation.

TABLE 8.3   Required Working Periods for Paid Annual Vacations

Working Period (WP)	Paid Annual Vacations
1 year $\leq$ WP $<$ 10 years	5 Days
10 years $\leq$ WP $<$ 20 years	10 Days
WP $\geq$ 20 years	15 Days

Payroll Distribution

By law, salaries should be paid at least once a month, and no later than the agreed-upon pay day. If the pay date falls on a weekend or public holiday, salaries should be paid in advance.

A Salary Handbook is required by the Shanghai Labor Bureau, (SLB) and by other cities such as Beijing and Suzhou. Hence, enforcement procedures vary from city to city. Every year in Shanghai, each company is required to conduct a salary registration estimate for the entire coming year, and report to the SLB. The company must adopt a new Salary Handbook yearly. If the total amount of salaries exceeds the amount originally registered, the company must report the new salaries to the SLB.

Salaries Paid in Foreign Currencies

Salaries paid in foreign currencies (to foreign employees only) are strictly controlled by the People's Bank of China (the central bank). Special documents must be submitted to the bank. Normally, they consist of the following:

1. The original passport
2. The original Employment Permit
3. The original Residence Permit
4. A copy of a valid Labor Contract (indicating the salary structure)
5. The Individual Income Tax (IIT) Receipt

Please note that even in Shanghai or Beijing, not all the local banks provide this service.

Employee Terminations

In recent years, rapid developments in major cities such as Beijing, Shanghai, and Guangzhou have led to very high employee turnover. Although employers may wish to have lower staff turnover, it is inevitable that for one reason or another, they will be faced with resignations and terminations. Strict rules and regulations need to be followed when an employee resigns or is being terminated.[2]

An employee needs to notify the employer 30 days in advance if he or she resigns. The advance notice should be three days for the probationary period.

An employer may terminate the labor contract if the employee does not meet job requirements during the probationary period, or if he or she materially breaches the employer's rules and regulations.

After the probationary period, if the employee is incompetent, and remains incompetent after training or a transfer to another position, the labor contract can also be terminated upon giving 30 days prior written notice, or one month's wages in lieu of notice.

Other rules and conditions also govern terminations. Note that an employer *cannot* terminate a labor contract if an employee:

- Is under medical observation
- Is suspected of having an occupational disease
- Has lost or partially lost work capacity due to an occupational disease or a work-related injury
- Is pregnant, confined after pregnancy, or nursing
- Has been working continuously for the employer for more than 15 years, and is less than five years from retirement age

When a foreigner has resigned from the employer, the Employment Permit and Residence Permit should be terminated with the Labor Bureau and Exit-Entry Administration Bureau. A temporary L visa (tourist visa) could be issued for a short-term stay in China.

Given the recent changes in the Labor Contract Law (see Chapter 9), there has been a shift toward the use of outsourcing service providers for functions such as accounting, tax, and other business processes (discussed in earlier chapters). Another trend is also developing; the use of placement staff or "people outsourcing" to meet such challenges. The next chapter will discuss this in greater detail.

Endnotes

1. Announcement No.20 in 2008, State Administration of Taxation. 国税发[2008]20号Order No.519, State Council of P. R. China. 国务院令第519号。
2. Labor Contract Law of P. R. China, January 1, 2008, 中华人民共和国劳动合同法.

9

The 2008 Labor Contract Law

On January 1, 2008, the Chinese government made a major addition, the Labor Contract Law, to its already substantial body of labor legislation. The new Labor Contract Law (LCL) was adopted on June 29, 2007.

Purpose and Effects of the New Labor Contract Law (LCL)

The LCL aims to improve job security for employees. The most significant impact is the adoption of an open-ended employment period for those who have completed two one-year terms with a company. The legislation limits overtime, sets minimum wages, and requires one month's pay for each year worked for its terminated or dismissed employees. All entities, regardless of the number of employees they have, are required to comply with the new law and regulations.

Many foreign companies have complained that the new law raises their labor costs. The open-ended term in the law has somewhat re-created the "iron-rice bowl," feared by many foreign businesses.

Some companies terminated contracts and asked employees to resign before the law went into effect. One of the largest Chinese makers of telecommunications equipment, in fact, recently offered about 7,000 employees new contracts with benefits when they terminated their old agreements. Many companies are also worried about the impact that the labor contract law has on their internal operations. The new labor contract law warrants detailed study by foreign companies doing businesses in China.

Written Employment Contract

The new law's single most important feature is that it requires a written labor contract. Ever since the opening up of the China economy 30 years ago, foreign businesses, particularly in the manufacturing sector, have been absorbing huge amounts of labor. Most of these people come from rural areas. They move to the cities to take up jobs. Before the new law came into effect, they were often less protected, in the sense that many companies might not provide written contracts to guide the terms of employment. Many of the unprotected employees could only rely on verbal promises about pay and terms of employment made to them when they were hired.

About the New Labor Contract Law

The new law now requires all labor contracts to be made in writing. It imposes significant penalties on employers who fail to comply. Employees also have a right to claim double payment for months worked without written contracts. This rule is targeted at companies that adopt informal employment relationships.

The law prescribes that the employer must present written labor contracts to employees within one month of establishing the employment relationship. If the employer fails to sign an employment contract with an employee within one year from the day the employee starts work, the employer shall be deemed to have entered into a non-fixed-term contract with the employee.

Termination

Prior to the new law, the length or period of employment for an employer with an employee was normally one year (known as one fixed-term). At the end of the term, the employer and employee could choose whether to renew the contract. If the employer decided not to renew the contract, even earlier than the end of the term, the notice period or compensation in lieu of notice period could be included as a way to terminate a contract.

However, under the new law, this arrangement is workable only for two fixed-term contracts; if the employer enters into a third consecutive fixed-term contract, the termination of an employee becomes more complicated.

Changes Stipulated by the New Law

Effectively, the new law allows for only two fixed-term renewals, after which the employment relationship has a non-fixed term, unless the employee breaches the employer's rules, commits a serious dereliction of duty, is incompetent, suffers a disability, or there is a major change in objective circumstances rendering the contract nonperformable.

Multinational foreign investment enterprises typically do not commit the types of labor violations that are most common in China. Therefore, it is unlikely that, at least initially, the law will alter significantly most of the labor practices of large foreign-based employers in China.

Under the old labor law, an employee could be discharged either at the expiration of a term contract or for cause. To avoid the need to terminate employee for causes, employers can choose to continuously hire employees under a series of short-term contracts. This practice is no longer possible under the LCL. The employer is only permitted to enter into a maximum of two term-contracts with the employee.

Employees can terminate the employment relationship on 30 day's notice for any reason, but they may also do so without notice if the employer fails to provide the working conditions specified in the labor contract, or does not pay salaries or social insurance premiums on time and in full, or issues rules and regulations that violate the law.

From the point of view of many employers, there is a bias against employers who wish to terminate employment contracts. While an employee has the choice of giving notice, an employer does not. This claim may be debatable since the employer is generally in the stronger position, but perhaps the pendulum has swung too much in favor of employees, creating an unfair situation. Since the start of the LCL on January 1, 2008, the job market has not been very positive. Employers are more reluctant to hire. At the very least, they are more cautious.

Probationary Period

The LCL imposes strict restrictions on probationary periods in employment relationships. Probationary periods are permitted, but their length is limited. The maximum probation period is based on the period of the contract. The probationary period is one month if the contract term is less than one year; two months if the contract period is less than three years; six months if the contract period is more than three years. The LCL requires employers to pay their employees at least 80 percent of their contractual salaries during the probationary period. It is expected that the penalties for violating these rules will increase, and that termination of contracts without notice or severance pay will become more difficult during the probationary period. The employer will have to prove that the employee has not fulfilled the recruitment conditions set out in the employment contract.

Employers have to be more careful when hiring new staff since they now have less flexibility. Even termination during the probationary period requires sufficient evidence. Furthermore, an employee is subject to only one probationary period by the same employer.

The law negates any agreement by which the prospective employer and employee might wish to deviate from the labor contract law. The law makes it impossible for a willing employer to make a new hire on terms that deviate from the law, even if a prospective employee is willing to accept something less than what the law requires. It is not surprising that the workers and employees are complaining about the bad effects of the LCL, despite its good intentions (弄巧反拙).

Non-Fixed-Term Contract

The LCL has numerous provisions designed to protect employees' rights and enhance job security. One key provision is that employees who have been employed at the same enterprise for 10 years or more will be legally entitled to a non-fixed-term employment contract, which should guarantee adequate financial compensation. Many employers panicked on learning of this provision and urged, bribed, or coerced long-serving employees to take early retirement or voluntary redundancy. As mentioned at the beginning of this chapter, the large telecommunications equipment manufacturing company persuaded about 7,000 employees who had been with the company for more than eight years to resign. In return, each of the employees received a lump sum of one month's salary for every year of employment, plus one additional month's salary, and were allowed to rejoin the company on short-term contracts.

Besides the fact that a continuous 10-year working period can lead to an open-term contract, there are further problems for employers. If an employee continues working after the expiration of his second term contract, the subsequent employment contract is also deemed to be a non-fixed-term contract. Under a non-fixed-term contract, the employee is employed until he chooses to terminate the contract, or reaches retirement age. The employer can only terminate the employment contract by discharging the employee for breach of contract.

It was common for foreign investors to find themselves in the midst of staff issues even prior to the passage of the LCL. It is also a common belief that foreign companies (外企) offer better terms, and generally comply with labor negotiations and laws. With the imposition of the LCL, however, more foreign companies may be reluctant to offer better terms to employees.

Noncompetition Agreement

The law allows an employer to specify noncompetition and confidentiality in the employment contract, or through a confidentiality agreement with an employee who bears the obligations of confidentiality and noncompetition. Such agreements require the employer to make compensation. The employer has to pay monthly compensation for the noncompetition period after the termination or ending of the employment contract. If the employee breaches the noncompetition restriction, he or she will have to pay the employer liquidated damages as agreed.

Many foreign employers require most or all of their Chinese employees to enter into noncompetition agreements that restrict their right to work for a competitor after termination of employment. The LCL imposes significant restrictions on these agreements. The most important restrictions are that noncompetition agreements cannot be imposed on all employees. Only senior management and other employees with access to critical trade secrets are required to enter into a noncompetition agreement. Once an employment contract is terminated or ends, the term of the noncompetition restriction should not exceed two years as it prohibits a person from serving with a competitor that produces or deals in the same type of product or engages in the same type of business as the employer, or prohibits him or her from opening his or her own business to produce or deal in the same type of product or engage in the same type of business.

The restriction must also be limited in geographic scope to a reasonable area, and the employer must pay compensation to the employee during the period that the noncompetition restriction is in effect.

The noncompetition and confidentiality clauses should be structured so as to protect the employer's business and trade. However, as the new labor contract law also imposes upon employers the implementation of the noncompetition and confidentiality requirements, there is very little room for employers and employees to negotiate with one another, even if they are willing. Consequently, many employers may become more reluctant to offer local Chinese employees training, and transmission of know-how, proprietary knowledge, and intellectual property. There are huge risks, given the requirements and protections to employees.

Employee Handbook and Establishment Procedures for an Employer's Internal Rules

All employers must maintain a written employee handbook setting out the basic rules and regulations of employment. This requirement applies to all companies, regardless of the size and number of employees. Failure to maintain an employee handbook means that an employer will effectively be unable to discharge employees for cause, since "cause" must be determined with reference to the employee handbook.

The law clarifies that the employer shall negotiate with employees or the employee representatives' congress, and shall bring forth schemes and opinions to stipulate internal rules on an equal basis, involving the following issues: remuneration, working hours, leave and holidays, labor security and sanitation, insurance and benefits, vocational training, labor discipline, and other matters.

Trade Unions

The LCL has reinforced the role of labor unions in safeguarding the legitimate rights and interests of employees in the following areas: (1) formulating corporate rules and bylaws; (2) bargaining on collective contracts; (3) providing opinions on mass payoffs; and (4) providing opinions on the termination of labor contracts.

The LCL requires employers to consult with unions in promulgating rules and regulations, concluding employment contracts, and implementing economic dismissals. This development comes on the heels of the 2004 Provisions on Collective Contracts issued by the Ministry of Labor and Social Security. However, given the historical tendency to be more concerned with maintaining production and employee discipline than employee rights, it remains unlikely in the near term that Chinese trade unions will transform themselves into vigorous employee advocates.

Despite this, just mentioning the words "trade unions" may lead foreign companies, especially U.S. and European ones, to refrain from hiring. Many of them have been too familiar with the negative effects that trade unions can have on an industry's production, at least from the employers' perspective.

Mass Layoffs

A change in the objective circumstances in which the employment contract was concluded is a legitimate basis for a mass layoff, which is defined as the need to lay off more than 20 or more employees, or more than 10 percent of total staff.

The law stipulates that the employer may lay off redundant employees, subject to mandatory procedures, under the following circumstances: (1) where the employer is restructuring in accordance with laws and regulations due to the bankruptcy of the enterprise; (2) where serious difficulties affect the production and management of the employer; (3) where the employer engages in a change of product line, or major technical renovation, or in a change of business model, and the employer still needs to lay off redundant employees after amendments to the original employment contract. One role that labor bureaus in China have traditionally played for foreign companies is to assist in the dismissal of employees when an employer reduces its workforce. The labor bureau, in effect, ensures that the employees do not demonstrate violently. The LCL carries forward this responsibility, but provides some protections for employees, such as the need for management to discuss layoffs with the labor union or employee representatives 30 days in advance; a prioritization of who should be retained if possible, such as those with long-term or non-fixed-term contracts, or those with children or elderly dependents; and the requirement to rehire dismissed employees if the rehiring occurs within six months of the layoff. Certain provisions of the 1995 Labor Law protecting employees from dismissal—for instance, if they have contracted an illness or are pregnant—are carried forward in the new legislation. Although management must go through the required consultative process, so long as the layoff is in accordance with the law, it would appear that the union or employees' representatives should not, at least in theory, be able to block the dismissal.

Severance

The LCL clarifies that severance should be equal to the employee's monthly remuneration, multiplied by the employee's number of years of service (any period of more than six months but less than one year will be counted as one year). The severance shall equal the employee's semi-monthly remuneration for employees whose service year is shorter than six months. Further, the law stipulates that the maximum amount should be three times the average city salary, with a 12-month cap.

A severance payment is required when the employer does not renew the fixed-term labor contract with the employee upon its expiration date, unless the employees refuse to extend the contract even under the same or better compensation package.

Some expatriate executives took notice of this provision and, when terminated in China, began to bring lawsuits in Chinese courts to collect for all their years of service to the company. But with the high salary received for work in China as a foreigner, the new law effectively precludes such suits (the same applies to highly paid Chinese citizens) by providing that, if the monthly salary is more than three times the average monthly salary in the local area, then the severance pay of that individual is limited to three times the average monthly wage in the local area.

Conclusion

The implementation of the new labor contract law is very recent. At the time of writing this book, it had been in effect for only eight months. There have been impact felt by both the employers and employees. Some good intentions may have produced unintended consequences. It is most likely that the Chinese government will need to look into the feedback and responses from various sources, including foreign companies. Fine-tuning and adjustments to the detailed rules and regulations will be necessary in the future.

10

Outsourcing

Outsourcing is not a new term in today's business world. It usually indicates when a company transfers a part of its business to another company—the service provider. In recent times, the term has been most commonly used for technology-related initiatives such as handing over the IT help desk to a third party. However, more and more businesses today are outsourcing their IT processes as well as other business-related services. These services are generally called business process outsourcing (BPO), which is typically reserved for noncore work. Examples of commonly outsourced business processes include Information Technology, Accounting and Finance, Sales and Telemarketing, and so forth.

Outsourcing as an Economic Option

From an economic standpoint, increasing productivity and lowering costs are essential elements for business success. Business process outsourcing usually can increase the business's competitive advantage. Outsourcing in the world today is seen as a strategic management option rather than just a cost-cutting operation. It aids companies to achieve their business objectives through operational excellence and a better market position. In order to compete in the global economy, companies today often outsource one or more of their operations. By utilizing business service providers strategically, senior management can bring better focus to their core business activities. This strategic shift is creating opportunities for businesses as a dynamic environment phenomenon. Furthermore, multinational use outsourcing as a tool to enhance and grow their businesses.

A recent report indicated that finance and accounting outsourcing has become a leading demand area in the second quarter of 2008. Demand for these services is particularly strong in Asia, Europe, the Middle East, and Africa.

As we have discussed in earlier chapters, the accounting, tax, and financial procedures and practices are very different and complex in China. For the CFO, outsourcing business and accounting processes are useful knowledge-sharing processes, not just means cutting costs. Selecting a service provider is one of the most important decisions a CFO has to make.

Outsourcing in China: A Catalyst for Business Success

Outsourcing in the financial field is nothing new. In the United States during the 1970s, it was common for computer companies to export their payrolls to outside service providers for processing. This continued into the 1980s when accounting services, payroll, billing, and word processing all became outsourced work. In addition to reducing costs, the main motive was to allow a company to invest more time, money, and human resources into core activities and building strategies. However, outsourcing financial and financial-related activities has especially extensive advantages. By outsourcing financial and accounting activities, companies can save a great deal of money since they do not need to set up a separate accounting department. Also, companies can save on labor management costs, including recruiting and training costs. Finance and accounting outsourcing also allows companies to take advantage of ready-trained professional labor. Last but not least, companies have the opportunity to access up-to-date technology, and improve their accounting management processes.

As a result, the CFO can enjoy flexibility in decision making, and companies are able to quickly set up operations or processes for other parts of the business. This is very important for CFOs, especially so for CFOs operating in China.

Legal Action

One U.S. NASDAQ company intended to establish a trading company in Shanghai. It hired a law firm, since the work of incorporating a company is normally undertaken by the legal counsel in the United States. However, the lawyer in Shanghai did not completely understand the business model of the company. He incorporated an IT technology and manufacturing company. The lawyer did not appreciate that the company's manufacturing processes were outsourced to an original equipment manufacturer (OEM). The company just required a trading license instead of a manufacturing license.

After its problems, the company went to a firm that was a true service provider for establishing and incorporating new entities, and it was able to help the company to amend the business scope to "trading company."

This case study illustrates that by outsourcing to the right service provider, the CFO can reduce human resource management costs, and have quicker access to specialized expert resources, more accurate process management, and support operations. In the long term, outsourcing noncore business activities can also lead to more predictable outcomes.

Global Trends with Regard to Outsourcing

Therefore, it is not surprising that many companies are outsourcing their accounting operations, especially when they expand their business across the globe. Some studies show that the global market for outsourcing finance and accounting operations is expected to grow at a 9.6 percent compounded annual growth rate and to exceed US$ 47.6 billion in 2008.

Recently, one of the biggest financial services providers in the world conducted a global survey of more than 300 companies to study the Asian outsourcing market. The survey focused mainly on outsourcing of business processes by small to medium enterprises (defined as those with turnover of US$ 500 million or less). Some of main findings from this survey are as follows:

- About one-third of these companies are outsourcing their accounting, debt collection, and tax processing. Outsourcing in Asia Pacific seems to have become more pervasive than generally thought.
- More than 45 percent of the companies in this survey with at least one office in China have already outsourced their financial functions. A further 30 percent of these companies are going to do so within the next three years, mainly because labor and operational costs are lower in Asian countries.
- When selecting service providers, one of the many important criteria is language. The majority of respondents (56 percent) say that language, and country as well as organizational culture strongly or very strongly dictate their outsourcing requirements. In addition to English as the most common business language, there is also a need to have staff who are fluent in other Asian languages.
- 54 percent of those surveyed believe outsourcing is an integral part of performance results and an important strategy for success; however, [the service to provider right from the start] it is especially important that the objectives of outsourcing are made clear.
- Companies are more comfortable now than in the past with the idea of entrusting some finance, accounting, and human resources functions to service providers in Asia.

Outsourcing of Accounting Processes

In the previous case study, the financial controller of the U.S. parent company began to realize that the consulting firm is a reliable accounting, book-keeping, and tax services provider. Its ability to communicate in English, and to translate technical accounting language from Chinese to English was especially important to her. Although the controller was born in Taiwan, she grew up in the United States. She speaks good Mandarin, but is most familiar with Western accounting practices. She feels very comfortable with allowing the firm to communicate and share ideas with her American colleagues.

Throughout the years, she and her colleagues in other divisions have explained their business models to the firm, which in turn has been able to share its expertise in Chinese and international accounting and tax practices.

In the past, companies have been reluctant to outsource finance and accounting functions, believing them to be critical to the business, or too embedded within the internal processes to extract separate without involving a great deal of effort and risk. However, this attitude has changed tremendously in the past 10 years. The change started because of globalization. Globalization developed first with the big multinational companies, and then filtered down to small and mid-size companies. With the globalization of mid-size companies, outsourcing has become an almost inevitable choice, especially for CFOs. When mid-size companies move to invest in a foreign country, they do not have the knowledge and capabilities to understand how to operate the tax, accounting, and financial aspects of their businesses. In addition, they need to start up quickly. Finally, they do not have the infrastructure and ability to carry the overhead that a global multinational could. Thus, outsourcing offers the CFO a way to transform finance and accounting functions. Today, finance and accounting outsourcing is widely recognized as an effective management tool. Ever since China's market opening in the early 1980s, many international companies have entered the country using this mode of operation.

Outsourcing Today

In China's economy today, outsourcing is no longer an option but a necessity. Tough market competition demands that management focus on core competencies. Many foreign companies' CFOs are therefore considering outsourcing various aspects of their inhouse operations. They have realized that outsourcing allows them to acquire local knowledge, break cultural barriers, acquire professional skills, and most fundamentally, overcome the language barrier very quickly.

Business service providers can meet the accounting, tax, financial management, and consulting needs of companies. Finance and accounting outsourcing companies can perform monthly, quarterly, and annual accounting and bookkeeping tasks, or can supplement a company's present staff to cut administrative time. This enables a company to concentrate on its core competencies, leaving the specialized support functions to professionals.

Service providers as outsiders provide a different perspective when they process certain functions of the business. They are sensitive to errors, and can assist with ambitious plans for improvement.

Financial and accounting outsourcing services enable the decision makers of the business to carefully weigh the financial status of the company, before deciding on further strategies and future courses of actions. Accounting details help a business owner uncover current financial trends and pinpoint arrears of profit or loss, in order to curtail loss-generating expenditures and increase investment in profit-making divisions.

The following is a list of the usual finance and accounting outsourcing services that a good service provider can offer:

- Design and set-up of accounting systems
- Assistance with accounting software
- Day-to-day bookkeeping
- Assistance with monthly and year-end closing
- Accounts payable processing
- Account reconciliations
- Depreciation schedules
- Cost accounting
- Credit control
- Financial statement preparation
- Tax compliance: VAT and Corporate Taxes
- Budgets and forecasting
- Account staff training
- Payroll and social contribution management
- Internal audits

Because many different types of services are available in the market, a CFO must consider the different cultural environment and practices in China. A CFO must understand why these services are so necessary since China applies its own rules and regulations, and changes them frequently. Some of the commonly outsourced financial functions are accounting and bookkeeping, cashier services, accounts payable functions, and tax planning and filing.

Accounting and Bookkeeping Process

It is beneficial to outsource financial and accounting functions at the beginning stages of the business. A newcomer needs access to local expertise to avoid any unnecessary corrective costs. Business service providers can assist in setting up customized accounting systems and procedures that integrate accounting processes with the home business infrastructure. They can also collect all relevant documents, examine them for adequacy and legality, perform bookkeeping according to prevailing China Accounting Standards, and deliver financial statements to the local Tax Authority in a timely manner. Following the client's specific requirements, the financial reports will be prepared according to different accounting standards (such as the International Financial Reporting Standards) so that the foreign headquarters can have an indepth understanding. Service providers also provide high-quality bookkeeping; the work is handled by a team of accounting professionals that possesses a level of expertise not normally found in small businesses. These accounting teams are well structured, consisting of a team leader and professionally-trained accountants. Such a structure ensures reliability, and establishes quality control procedures.

Outsourcing accounting functions can also be seen as a way to prevent embezzlement, and other kinds of financial fraud that are perhaps the common fear of foreign investors and CFOs. Small businesses tend to fall prey to such crimes because they often do not have adequate controls in place. These controls include complete recording of all the accounts receivables and payables, proper reconciliation of accounts, authority and payment approval controls, and bank account reconciliation.

Sealed Matter

One client approached a consulting firm when he first set up his trading company. He was looking to outsource his accounting process because he was not familiar with the Chinese reporting requirements. However, he later hired an inhouse accounts assistant to carry out the work. Initially there was no problem, because at the start-up stage, the company did not face any complex situation. However, when activities became more complex, the client found that the inhouse accountant could not handle more complex issues such as VAT. Worse still, the accounts assistant was the custodian of the companys seals and stamps, and she wanted to triple her salary. She threatened to harm the company by using those seals and stamps (that represent the company).

Cashier Function

The cash and treasury functions are crucial in any business. The person who is recruited must have high integrity, a good personality, and strong technical competency. Good internal control procedures are also critical. Whenever a business first starts up, it is hard to find a reliable cashier, especially when the management team is not familiar with the business environment in China. This is when outsourcing the cashier function may be a better option than keeping it inhouse. The service provider can monitor bank movement, provide cash flow analysis, and raise any significant issues when necessary. The service provider can also be fully under the authority and control of the parent investor company in terms of cash management and cash handling, a great comfort to the investor.

Accounts Payable Outsourcing

For the sake of efficient internal control, a number of multinational corporations prefer to have a function process within the department that is being outsourced. Outsourcing accounts payable, for instance, allows a company to be less susceptible to fraud and control weaknesses because of the natural segregation of duties between inhouse personnel and third-party service providers.

Outsourcing accounts payable can have several additional benefits. Through the service provider, the CFO can ensure that there is more centralized control over payables despite different actual physical locations. It also can eliminate the headache of recruiting, hiring, and managing clerical staff, thus allowing management to focus on core strategic business operation.

Tax Regulation

Chinese tax authorities require all companies to file their company income tax on a quarterly basis, and the employees' individual tax filings on a monthly basis. Failure to do so may result in late interest charges and penalties. At the same time, most companies require that reports on these financial figures be sent back to the home country headquarters to update them on how well the China businesses are doing. To provide prompt, fairly presented financial statements is critical for smooth operations.

This is one of the major advantages of outsourcing finance and accounting services. It is especially apparent when filing tax returns and auditing the financial records of a company. The service provider ensures that the parent company has all its financial records in place for ready reference at the time of filing taxes. This transparency also brings the company a good reputation among auditors and financial institutions. Also, most accounting outsourcing providers customize their services for individual clients. Hence, a business can rest assured that its records are up to date and accurate, and have been kept in complete confidence.

One very important reason for outsourcing tax compliance to a good service provider is that the provider can communicate with the local tax authorities effectively when tax issues arise during the course of business operations, tax audits, or business audits. For example in Shanghai, there are more than 20 local district tax authorities, and a business needs to report to a local tax authority based within the business location.

There are no simple criteria for deciding between outsourcing functions and handling them inhouse. The benefits associated with outsourcing are numerous, and one should consider each project on its individual merits. Ongoing operational costs that may be avoided by outsourcing are also critical when making a decision. Outsourcing should allow organizations to be more efficient, flexible, and effective, while reducing costs.

Some of the key advantages brought by outsourcing include the following:

- Staffing flexibility
- High-caliber professionals that hit the ground running
- Ability to tap into best practices
- Knowledge transfer to permanent staff
- Cost-effective and predictable expenditures
- Access to the flexibility and creativity of experienced problem solvers
- Sharper focus on resource and core competency

Other Considerations: Problems in Outsourcing

Despite the numerous benefits of outsourcing, particularly for foreign companies operating in China, there are also limitations that a CFO must consider at the same time. For instance, is a good service provider available? Is the quality of services up to expectations? Some CFOs believe that activities such as strategic planning, risk management, and other issues are strategic to the company, and should be handled inhouse.

The main issue with outsourcing in China can be the language barrier. There is a wide diversity of languages and cultures in China, and there are not many vendors that have a presence in each of the different jurisdictions. A CFO might initially want to outsource everything to one company, but what if that company does not have offices in every area of China? For this reason, some CFOs prefer to rely on two or three service providers.

In order to avoid these outsourcing problems, a company should take preventive actions, and adopt a thorough selection process for the service provider. The CFO should maintain close contact and control of the outsourced operations, and keep up to date with all issues concerning the outsourced operation.

Sourcing the Outsourcing: Select the Business Partner

Accounting is one aspect of business that needs to be handled with extreme care and caution, because the very backbone of the company depends on it. Each financial transaction can change the final profit and loss of the business. Hence, all transactions, whether in cash or credit, need to be accounted for by the accounting division. It is crucial to identify the most appropriate business partner for a company's financial and accounting outsourcing.

We use the term *business partner* because a CFO who is making a selection needs to view a service provider as a true partner that will support the parent company. Strategic outsourcing is not a short-term endeavour. It provides companies with both long-term and short-term gains. These benefits are best realized by selecting a provider who brings value rather than one who offers the lowest prices.

Areas critical to the success of an outsourcing program are as follows:

- Understanding company goals and objectives
- A strategic vision and plan
- Selecting the right vendor

- Ongoing management of relationships
- A properly structured contract

A CFO should ask these questions when deciding on strategic outsourcing:

- Which business activity should we outsource?
- Who should our service provider be?
- How should we manage the project?
- How should we agree on payment terms?
- How can we achieve the desired results?

By intelligently choosing a provider that matches its skill requirements, and carefully detailing and outlining its project requirements, a company can ensure that it can meet these requirements within budget.

Four main steps are critical in selecting a service provider. (1) management has to identify the objectives of outsourcing. Is it to be more focused on core business, cost cutting, or better internal control procedures? (2) Management must identify what finance and accounting functions to outsource. As mentioned earlier in this chapter, according to the size of businesses and their specific needs, companies can choose to completely outsource the financial processes, or only certain functions within the financial process. To decide this, a CFO may wish to consider how closely must the finished work from the business provider be integrated into the headquarters' reports. (3) Once the objectives and the financial functions that need to be outsourced are identified, the company can go on to select the service provider. This will be the most important step, since it is always time consuming to transfer information to the service provider for the work. (4) In China, there are many service providers in the market, and service fees vary; however, a CFO must find the most appropriate service providers for the company's needs: not only in terms of language capability and technical knowledge, but also in terms of cultural knowledge and professionalism. In order to find the most suitable service provider, CFOs usually look at the following criteria to make their selections.

1. *Reference Check.* Request to see examples of previous work, and a client list, if it is available. First, the sample shows how well the

provider does its work, and the list shows their position in the market. These sources also reveal whether the firm has the relevant experience to meet its clients' needs.

2. *Nature and Scope of the Services.* A good business service provider should be equipped with technical knowledge. It should also provide a full suite of accounting services. For example, a service provider of bookkeeping services must have the knowledge and execution capabilities for company compliance, accounting, payroll, tax, and audit. This will save a company the effort of finding and coordinating different service providers. A full-scale service provider will also be able to point out when an issue requires an extension of services. The provider can also add value by alerting the company to any potential problems.

3. *Technical requirements.* A good service provider should be familiar with the different financial and accounting rules and regulations, and be able to prepare the work consistent with its client's or its headquarters' requirements. For instance, an American company with a subsidiary in China may want its financial reports in two formats for consolidation purposes, one in accordance with Chinese Accounting Standards, and the other in United States Generally Accepted Accounting Principles.

4. *International Presence.* A multinational business must have a service provider with a good international presence. No company wants to go through the selection and communication processes with different firms from different countries.

5. *Professionalism: Security and Privacy.* This is a critical element in choosing the right service provider. You will be sending vital data, and you need to make sure that security infrastructures in their locations adequately meet your needs.

6. *Price.* There are two pricing models; one that goes by an hourly rate, or the other that goes by a monthly rate, based on the client's requirements. Although price is a consideration, it is important not to make it the basis of your decision. Most of the time, the prices are set for specific reasons. Before hiring the service provider with the lowest quote, the CFO needs to consider the quality of the services provided.

7. *Response Time.* The service provider must also be able to respond to you quickly.

8. *Qualifications.* A qualified service provider in China is awarded a certificate of qualification from the government authorities. In Shanghai, for example, a provider must be certified by the Shanghai Finance Bureau as a qualified accounting, bookkeeping, and related accounting services company. Always check such certificates to ensure that the service provider is legally and professionally registered.

9. *Trust Relationship.* A high level of trust is required for financial and accounting outsourcing, because the relationship involves financial information, and even actual cash transfers. A study by a financial services company indicates that 40 percent of companies that currently outsource accounting services characterize their relationship as a partnership, while 29 percent describe it as one between buyer and vendor.

As soon as a service provider is selected, communication with the service provider should begin. This is the time for the client to express its expectations, and instruct the provider on how best to meet its requirements. This is also the time to evaluate the quality of services, and to see how well the service provider is coordinating with internal employees.

Outsourcing Trends in China

There are lots of global predictions that expect a healthy growth rate in business process outsourcing (BPO) markets. The forecast for the Chinese market is one of tremendous growth, far beyond earlier expectations: not only in the traditional outsourcing sectors, such as manufacturing and information technology, but also in BPO services. Companies in China are becoming more comfortable with the idea of entrusting some finance, accounting, and other related functions to outsiders. There is also an increasing demand for foreign businesses to outsource their noncore business functions, to focus and do battles more effectively in the competitive markets.

BPO is gradually becoming known as knowledge process outsourcing (KPO), since it involves knowledge-intensive business processes that require significant domain expertise, analytical skills, and judgment capabilities. Unlike traditional BPOs where relatively low-level skills were required, here knowledge and professional education are the key. KPO providers typically offer high-end services in almost all industries. Several countries are now trying to build capabilities in specific KPO areas. For example, Russia claims to be a good destination for healthcare industry outsourcing services, while China has established itself as a place to outsource financial services. In the coming years, we will see far greater demands for both traditional outsourcing and knowledge-process outsourcing.

11

Risk Management and Internal Audit

Risks are inherent in all businesses, but risk management can be successful only if it is integrated into the business strategy and operations of a company. Many companies, big and small, have invested significant resources to manage risks. Successful risk management must also mean a good balance between the costs of implementing a good risk management system, and achieving the returns that the business wishes to reap. For foreign companies investing and doing business in China, risk management must be a clearly focused strategy of managing the risks associated with entering the Chinese market. In most cases, for big and small companies, the first questions to ask are: What is the loss of not doing business in China? What will the company gain or lose? The economic growth in China for the last 30 years along with the tremendous market potential, and competition from other players have made matters very clear for foreign investors: Whatever the risks may be, one must do business in China. Foreign businesses, and especially their CFOs, need to manage these risks when doing business in China.

Risk Management in China

Since we must conduct business in China, how do we manage enterprise risks when operating there? How would international CFOs see the risk management of a subsidiary company doing business there? This book provides CFOs with a guide and framework for enterprise risk management. This chapter concentrates on internal controls, and the internal audit aspects of risk management.

Regulatory and Compliance Risks

Going international and coming to China mean facing the challenges of numerous complex regulations. We have covered the various compliance requirements throughout this book. These compliance issues relate to human resource employment, taxation, foreign exchange, business scope and capabilities, and so forth.

It is clear to many foreign investors that China has improved greatly in terms of compliance enforcement. The next 30 years of continuous economic growth will, no doubt, accelerate the speed of this inevitable development.

Some foreign investors, even today, are quite oblivious to compliance risks, claiming that China locals themselves are not "compliant" in certain areas. They ignore the fact that, as foreign investors, they are not locals. Fortunately, such investors are becoming rare.

Global Integration

China has become intertwined and integrated with the world economy. Like India, it has become an economic powerhouse that is also vulnerable to global events and risks such as oil price rises, the U.S. subprime financial crisis, escalation of food prices, and so forth. It is crucial to understand how China's economic risks are correlated to the rest of the world.

Many Chinese worry about the impact of the U.S. subprime crisis. Worries extend to how the crisis will affect foreign businesses (especially local and foreign financial institutions) operating in China. Will these companies cut back on expansion and hiring? Will they even retrench staff in China?

Some are even worried that the property meltdown could even be replicated to some extent in China. Many have commented that there is an obvious property bubble in Tier One cities like Guangzhou, Shenzhen, Shanghai, and even Beijing. The only reason, as some people have pointed out, the bubble has not burst because of the 2008

Beijing Olympic Games in China. Naturally, we will have to wait to see how developments pan out. All these issues point to the simple fact that the China of today can no longer be disassociated from the rest of the world.

Chinese Consumers

The vastness of China's consumer market presents tremendous opportunities. However, it also poses great risks and challenges. One very good example is the one-child policy. There is a growing worry about the continual sustainability of the property market. It is an undeniable fact that property prices should be sustained through continued economic growth, which in turn is dependent on a productive population. The one-child policy, coupled with an aging population, explains why more people may be worrying about the sustainability of the consumer market.

The huge consumer market in China must be looked upon from both the positive and negative aspects. There are many foreign investors who are easily fascinated by the millions of people in a given city. However, there are also dependencies that are built into such market sizes. By the time these are analyzed, it may be too late to spread out such a customer-dependent risk.

Competition

China's huge market has attracted businesses and inventors from all over the world. Big and small companies are competing aggressively here. In fact, it has been said that the big will not always beat the small, but that the fast will always beat the slow. This context highlights a point that often arises with Singapore companies. On many occasions, we hear Singapore business people make comments like: "In Singapore, we do not have such issues, and people will do things this way or that way."

Many Singapore companies easily forget that they are competing in a much bigger market such as Shanghai, where the population is about 18 million. Competitors come from all over the world. Consumers are largely Chinese from the North, South, East, and West, as well as many foreigners living in China. Hence, the spectrums of tastes, behaviors, preferences are wide.

It is, therefore, essential not to carry over home country assumptions into China. Smart competitors will certainly not do that. This is not to say, however, that experiments in the home country cannot be adapted to suit competition in China.

Other Specific Risks

There are many other specific risks that we cannot list exhaustively. The CFO must be able to identify specific risks that affect his company's business. The CFO must structure and manage two sorts of risks:

- Strategic risk management (as mentioned above)
- Operational risk management

In China, in addition to identifying strategic business risks, the CFO must develop a risk-management framework to control and manage operational risks.

Many MNCs and other large enterprises possess huge resources to develop and implement risk-management systems. This chapter provides pointers to small businesses on managing operational risks.

For small companies, the various chapters of this book provide CFOs with an insight on the feel of the various aspects of operating a business in China: for example, business incorporation, labor rules, financial and tax regulations, and so forth. The general framework is very important. A CFO can be lost without such knowledge.

Internal Control System

The CFO must understand that many things are changing very fast in China. So the risk factors move very quickly. With changes in information technology, such risk patterns will change even faster. Since the Chinese subsidiary is far away from the parent company, the issues become even more critical.

It is imperative that the CFO of a small business be able to build an adequate internal control system for its business. The internal control system of any organization should also give due considerations to the cultural and regulatory differences of China. For a small business without huge resources, how does a CFO build such an internal control system? One of the key solutions is for a CFO to use an outsourced consultant. The outsourced consultant can help the CFO to structure his subsidiary's internal control processes and procedures. A good outside consultant will be very familiar with the various aspects of internal controls that a small foreign business in China needs. In addition, the consultant can also constantly update changes in regulations that will impact the operations of internal control. The key is for the CFO to maintain regular communication with the outside consultant.

The Importance of Human Resources

Besides using an outside consultant, the CFO needs to consider the people in the company very carefully. Many foreign CFOs operating in China (especially for smaller companies) feel that because they have a small company with only a small number of people, they must place a lot of trust on just those few people. Although companies often face limited personnel resources, this situation has created a tremendous amount of risk, because the company places such a huge reliance on only a few people. As mentioned earlier, one of the answers to this problem is to segregate functions, procedures, and processes among internal people and outside service providers. This allows the CFO to diversify the risk of being dependent on only a few people in the organization. The next thing that the CFO needs to do when building the internal control system for a small company is to ensure that there is constant communication with the local site people. Communications can be done through frequent teleconferencing, and crucial preliminary meetings when a company is first being set up. The CFO should take an active role to ensure that internal control procedures and policies are being drilled into the company. Through this reporting mechanism and communications, the CFO will be able to understand directly how the business is functioning. At the same time, in case of any trouble, the system should be able to alert the CFO at the very first instance.

Internal Audit Functions

Many companies will adopt internal audit functions and procedures. MNCs are accustomed to parachuting internal auditors from home countries to carry out internal audits for subsidiaries in China. This is the normal behavior of MNCs as well as mid-size companies. When such MNCs parachute their internal auditors to China, one of the key objections or comments of their local site general managers or CEOs is that "China is very different." CEOs and general managers arduously try to explain to their head offices that practices and procedures in China are very different. There is always a difference in perception between local site managers, CFOs, and internal auditors.

Self Supervision

A service provider was tasked to act as an internal auditor for an agricultural company. This company owns and operates fruit plantations. It hires contract farmers to work on the plantation to grow fruit. The farmers were paid daily rates, depending on the hours they worked a day, and the number of days they worked in a month.

The farmers were very concerned about their pay, as well as that of the other farmers. They needed to be assured that they were all being treated fairly. Normally, the salary of each farmer would be considered confidential.

Therefore, when the service provider was auditing this company, it was very keen to understand how the company maintained salary confidentially among the farmers. To its surprise, the company adopted a very open system. The service provider understood from the management that in the plantation where all the farmers worked, everybody knew who was present or absent from work on any particular day. The system was one of self-supervision among the farmers. Obviously, the company also had a system that recorded the attendance of each farmer. At the end of each month, the company generated a list showing the number of days in the month that each farmer had worked, the salary each farmer draws in that month. In fact, it allowed everyone to know each other's pay. If someone did not work on a certain day, but received extra pay even though he was absent, the matter would definitely be reported to the management in the form of a complaint against the company.

The internal audit function is normally seen as the fulfillment of internal management purposes only. However, when foreign businesses operate in China, many of the external influences impact the company directly. Therefore, when internal auditors audit their subsidiaries, they need to know a fair amount about how a company operates in China. Internal auditors of companies cannot understand internal audit workings unless they know what the company actually experiences in China. At the very minimum, they must have a basic understanding of how the company was formed in China, as well as basic understanding of the tax structure and the labor regulations in the country. Without some basic understanding of such matters, the internal auditor may find it very difficult to carry out his or her role, and communicate with local site managers. It is also wrong to assume that understanding such matters is the responsibility of the external auditor only.

In the case study above, we highlighted how the management of the China farm adopted a system that was fair, open, and unique. Confidentiality, in fact, was not the primary concern here. Fair and open treatment was the key consideration. Thus, the internal audit function in China requires internal auditors to have a fairly good understanding of how businesses and people behave in different environments. Much of what we see in the world outside of China may not be applicable there.

Sarbanes-Oxley

Part of the internal audit requirements are the Sarbanes-Oxley (SOX) requirements for U.S. public companies. These typically affect material subsidiaries of U.S. companies that are operating in China. If these subsidiaries are material to the balance sheet of the parent company, the SOX regulations require them to be audited, and to pass the related tests of internal controls.

Although the U.S. headquarters sends out auditors to China to enforce the SOX requirements on their China subsidiaries, the auditors must work with due consideration of the many situations unique in China. In one example, a service provider had been assigned to carry out one aspect of the internal audit on a restaurant. The emphasis was on segregation of duties and revenue collections. The company could not explain why the daily collections were lower than expected, even though the restaurant experienced huge crowds.

When the SOX template and control testing procedures were carried out (just on those aspects), they indicated that there were also segregation of duties. So where was the revenue leakage?

The investigation did not stop at SOX documentation alone, since there was a belief that there could be collusion. Through further investigations and checks, the service provider discovered that "transaction slips" were being utilized multiple times, and were not recorded into the system. The transaction slips were being "flown back" onto patrons' table and recycled. In China, this practice is prevalent in food and beverages outlets. The practice of "flying back" the slips is known as 飞单. It is very common because customers do not normally ask for tax invoices. The team of people in this particular case was systematically replaced. Such situations are especially pervasive, in major cities of China, such as Shanghai and Beijing. To encourage patrons to acquire tax invoices (发票) on settlement of bills, the Tax Authority created a "sort of lottery participation" on the tax invoice. Each tax invoice contains a "scratchable portion." The patron can scratch the portion that may reveal a prize, normally ranging from RMB 10 to bigger amounts such as RMB 50 or RMB 100. This is unique in China. The system indirectly enhances controls, and enforces better tax collections.

From the above case study, it is very important to consider the unique requirements of China's culture, procedures, and systems. Therefore, it is incorrect to assume that if an auditor has done SOX audit work for a U.S. subsidiary, he or she can easily apply the same methods to a China subsidiary. The documentation, training, implementation, review, and solutions recommendations will have to be considered in the context of China.

If a foreign business operating in China has a parent company that is a public company in the United States, and if the subsidiary is outsourcing to a service provider, SOX requirements would also entail that the service provider be SAS70[1] (Statements of Accounting Standards 70) qualified under the American standards of accounting. SAS70-qualified service providers can ensure that SOX controls and requirements are in place when outsourcing for subsidiaries of public companies. This is especially important as an increasing number of subsidiaries in China are becoming more material to their parent companies in the United States.

Corporate Governance

This chapter has discussed issues relating to building internal control systems and carrying out internal audit functions. It is also very important to consider corporate governance in the total context of risk management. This is even more important when doing business in China. Specifically relating to corporate governance are the appointment of key personnel, the governance of the stamps and seals of a company, as well as corporate governance procedures. Risk management, together with corporate governance, has to be looked upon in its entirety. Corporate governance requirements pose strong challenges to small businesses. Not only do business owners have to be involved in day-to-day commercial operations, they are also faced with the challenge of not having enough time and resources to manage corporate governance. We have mentioned the critical risk of relying on one or two local employees to manage such matters, and hoping that nothing will go wrong. The case studies in this chapter demonstrate that such reliance can give rise to a great deal of corporate-governance risk, exposures, and other business risks. So, how should a small business handle corporate governance? We emphasize this because there are many small firms doing business in China. Hence, it is important that CFOs look toward good outside consultants for the services that guard against corporate governance risks. CFOs will be able to sleep better once they find good consultants to whom they can outsource these procedures and processes.

Endnote

1. Statement on Auditing Standards No. 70: This is an auditing statement issued by the Auditing Standards Board of the American Institute of Certified Public Accountants (AICPA). It defines the professional standards used by a service auditor to assess the internal controls of a service organization, and issue a service auditor's report. There are two types of service auditor reports (AICPA Audit Guide: Applying SAS No. 70, as Amended).

12

Expanding Across China

China offers a huge market. With a population of 1.3 billion and counting, it makes perfect sense that all foreign businesses want access to the entire market. Localization plays an extremely important role in any business strategies, and this means that it is essential to expand and move across China.

Many foreign operations that are not successful in the first one to three years will wrap up their businesses and head home. Very often, if they are forced by circumstances, they will come back to China later. It is also very typical of operations that are established and stable by the end of the second and third year to start looking around, to replicate and expand across other parts of China. We have seen examples of many multinational firms expanding into the most rural and less developed areas of China, just to be near their desired market. For example, 3M has offices in the far western region of Urumqi (沈阳) just to be near their customers.

The prospect of expanding fast is one temptation that must be handled with care. This is where most risks set in. China is huge geographically, and as previous chapters have already mentioned, cultures and behaviors differ as well. This is also true of business practices; they can differ in different places. Many foreign businesses assume that any part of China will accept the same practices. What is acceptable and may work in Shanghai, may not be applicable in Urumqi (乌鲁木齐) or Shenyang (沈阳). Details, cultures, tastes, and behaviors can be very diverse, and these have direct implications for business expansions. Although there are replicable similarities that can be utilized while expanding across China, even a totally homogenous business can be subjected to many variables. It is only safe to say that in China, variables are integral factors that are not to be ignored. When a business expands, it must adjust and acclimatize to the local area of operations.

Business Dynamics

A Singaporean business person was a classic example of one who made the common mistake of neglecting these precautions when expanding across China. He wanted to establish food courts (食閣) in Dalian, located in the northeastern region of China, after the initial success he had experienced in Shanghai. Food courts are designated places for hawkers to set up stalls to sell various items. Food courts are usually set up in very comfortable surroundings, and are highly popular in Singapore. A very large compound was rented, and the many different types of Singapore and Southeast Asian cuisine were available.

However, the food turned out to be disappointing to the northeastern Chinese people. Even though the food was of just as high quality as the ones in Shanghai and Singapore, consumers never liked the concept.

People in the northeastern part of China like food in huge portions, unlike the small portions that were served in the food courts. The taste of the Singaporean and Southeast Asian food was also too different from northeastern food. Clearly, the business venture failed to understand that the expansion from Shanghai to Dalian involved new business dynamics and requirements. There are many unseen variables to consider when expanding across China.

Expansion in China Is Not as Easy as You Think

Expansion in China is never an easy task. The sheer vastness of China's geography, together with the diversity that ranges throughout, regardless of whether it is culture or business practices, makes expansions tricky and difficult. As the case studies show, it is important not to be lured by the simple potential of the Chinese market. Options must be weighed carefully together with all the possible pitfalls, and planning must be done before expanding across China. When foreign invested enterprises (FIEs) plan to expand their business in other Chinese cities, there are three common approaches: Liaison Office, Branch Company and Subsidiary Company.

Sweet Success

On the other hand, there are classic examples of foreign business that have successfully integrated the cross-border variables into their ventures across China. One good example is another Singaporean restaurant in Shanghai.

This Singaporean restaurant has been in China for almost five years; it sells all the original dishes that are found in Singapore, and is highly popular, and always crowded. Examining the crowd that patronizes the restaurant, it is safe to say that more than 70 percent of the customers are not from Singapore. The Chinese, especially people from Shanghai, greatly value customer service. At any one time, one of the two bosses of the restaurant is around to meet all his customers. This creates excellent rapport between the customers and the restaurant. On top of this, the food that is served maintains the original taste, with a slight variation (additional sweetness) to suit the taste buds of the locals. People from Shanghai also enjoy having their food served in multiple small portions, which is identical to how Singaporean and Southeast Asian cuisine is served. The owners of this foreign business have factored in all the variations into their planning, enhancing their chances of success in their business foray into and across China.

Liaison Office

Before 2005, many FIEs established Liaison Offices ("联络办事处"), as the frontline offices in cities such as Beijing, Shanghai, Tianjin, Shenzhen, or Suzhou. Compared with the Representative Office (RO) of a foreign company, the Liaison Offices are governed by the FIEs in China rather than the parent company directly. While capable of handling market research, sourcing, project investigation, customer liaison, the Liaison Offices cannot conduct businesses directly. There is also no requirement for capital injection. In this respect, the Liaison Offices and Registered Office (驻中国代表处) are the same.

From 2006 onwards, however, with the promulgation of the newly amended Company Law and the Company Registration Regulations, both effective January 1, 2006, the concept of the Liaison Office is no longer applicable. According to the Law of the PRC on Administrative Permits, effective July 1, 2004, administrative authorities in China have been granting only those administrative permits that have a clear legal basis. This may be seen as a signal that the administration of Liaison Offices has changed.

Meanwhile, according to the Company Registration Regulations, all the entities that conduct business activities outside the location of the legal address shall be required to register with the local Administration of Industry and Commerce (AICs). Those conducting business activities without any approval from the AICs, or the Tax Bureau will be deemed to be operating illegally, and will be penalized by the authorities. Hence, we may conclude that the Liaison Offices are no longer allowed for foreign businesses.

This view is also backed up by the provisions of the Circular on Legal Implementation Issues on Company Registration Regulations of Foreign Invested Enterprise (Circular AIC WAI QI ZI [2006] No. 81). In this Circular, local AICs in China have stopped accepting the registration applications of Liaison Offices, and will not renew existing Liaison Office registrations when their terms expire. Existing Liaison Offices may choose to deregister, or apply to set up new branch companies based on the actual business scheme after their current terms expire.

Liaison Offices have become a thing of the past. The reason for this is local bureaucratic policy. In the eyes of the local tax bureau, the Liaison Offices cannot bring in tax revenue even though they utilize many local resources. In addition, it is difficult to monitor and govern those Liaison Offices without any clear legal basis.

Branch Company

FIEs that have, or are planning to establish Liaison Offices have the option to establish branch companies. Any FIE whose registered capital has been paid up, and is in normal business operation may set up branch companies in accordance with relevant provisions of the State Administration of Industry and Commerce (SAIC). FIEs should avoid operating unregistered offices when the terms of their liaison offices expire, since they will encounter difficulties in submitting proper registration documents for various mandatory filings with the tax and labor authorities. These could also cause them to be penalized by the AIC.

An FIE may set up a branch company by incorporating the corresponding provision into its *Articles of Association*, and obtaining approval from the Ministry of Commerce or Foreign Economics Relationship and Trade Commission (the local agency of MOFCOM). The same paperwork has to be done with the local AIC before obtaining the formal Business License of Branch Company.

Branch companies can make their own decisions as long as they do not exceed the scope of the parent company's business operations. Branch operations must not exceed the powers and responsibilities of the company. As a nonindependent legal entity, all the legal responsibilities and liabilities of the branch company will be subject to the parent company in any situation.

There are two types of branch companies that can be registered according to the Chinese law:

- An independent accounting branch company
- A nonindependent accounting branch company

The main difference between an independent and a nonindependent accounting branch company is the degree of dependence on the parent company. While the nonindependent accounting branch is completely dependent on the parent company in all matters, the independent accounting branch company has a certain degree of independence. On the surface, the licenses obtained by the independent branch company and the nonindependent branch company, such as the Business License and Tax Registration Certificate, are the same. The major distinguishing difference is that the Tax Declaration Form to be submitted is quite different.

Independent Branch Company

Just as its name implies, an independent branch company is characterized by a certain degree of independence from the parent company. This independence is expressed through various ways:

- *Management.* There is a branch manager who represents the branch company in its business. The branch manager reports to the Board of Directors of the parent company.
- *Capitalization.* The branch company possesses its own working capital. However, the working capital is not the same as the Registered Capital. Branch companies, either independent or non-independent, are not required to inject any capital. In practice, the parent company can remit funds for the branch's normal operations.
- *Accounting.* The branch company has its own accounting team and prepares its own annual financial statements which will subsequently be consolidated with its parent's.
- *Tax duties.* The branch company shall be subject to limited tax duties.

Despite its independence, the branch company is a "part" or "branch" of the parent company, and is not a separate legal entity. Its inner constitution and its business relationships are based on the legal form of the parent company. Due to its business nature, the independent accounting branch company cannot enjoy the benefit of certain policies, such as tax incentives or tax exemptions.

There are some rules to follow:

- The parent company shall adopt Board of Directors Resolutions to illustrate that the intention of setting up a branch company has been agreed to by the directors.
- Based on the above BOD Resolutions, the parent company revises the *Articles of Association*, and prepares relevant necessary documents accordingly.
- An independent branch company is to obtain the preliminary approval by the AIC where the parent company is located.
- After completing the paperwork at the AIC where the parent company is located, an independent branch company must also announce its business at the local business registration government. That means that all the registration information of branch company will be listed on the local Administrations for Industry and Commerce (AICs) where the branch company is located.
- The branch company will have the exact name as the parent company, including the legal form annex without changes. For instance, if the name of the parent company is "AAA Ltd.," the

name of branch company located in Shanghai shall be "AAA Ltd Shanghai Branch Company.

Nonindependent Branch Company

The Nonindependent Branch Company is easier to understand. It is, by no means, independent of the parent company. There is no capitalization requirement, no independent business, and no independent accounting. The nonindependent branch company is only geographically, but by no means organizationally, separate from the parent company. It deeply relies on the parent company's structure and business. A nonindependent branch company is not allowed to be set up freely. It will need to be approved by the local AICs: that is, the AICs where the headquarters is located, and the AIC at the branch company location.

Tax Influences of Branch Structure

The tax consequences for an FIE of operating through branches may differ markedly from the consequences of operating through liaison offices. FIE headquarters established in low-tax districts in China may subsequently set up nonindependent branches to provide research and development, after-sales assistance, or other services from locations in nearby higher-tax districts, or in other cities. Although this practice has been targeted in the past by notices of the State Administration of Taxation, nonindependent branches cannot invoice customers, and therefore generally cannot be expected to pay enterprise income tax (EIT), business tax (BT), or value added tax (VAT). All billings to customers are carried out at the headquarters. All taxes are levied at the headquarters' rate and paid to the tax bureaus at the location of the headquarters, which may additionally offer local incentives, partially offsetting the FIE's obligations. Independent branches, however, can invoice customers and are subject to tax on their activities. The following rules govern the relationship between an FIE headquarters and its branches.

Enterprise Income Tax (EIT)

A headquarters and its branches are required to pay EIT on a consolidated basis to the tax bureau where the headquarters is located.

If different EIT rates apply to the headquarters and the branches, EIT should be calculated according to the respective rates where the income is generated, and paid centrally by the headquarters.

Business Tax (BT)

BT is payable to the local tax bureau by the office that renders the service. BT is generally not applicable to intracompany administrative services that are not invoiced (such as human resources or accounting services). However, if a branch provides services within its scope of business to its headquarters (such as research and development), it should charge for such services and pay BT.

An independent accounting branch company (see later paragraphs) is able to issue its own billings, and hence is required to pay local BT.

VAT

Where a taxpayer (1) maintains two or more establishments; (2) practices unified accounting; and (3) moves goods from one establishment to another to be sold; a sale of goods will be deemed to have occurred between the establishments for purposes of VAT, if the establishments concerned are located in different districts. VAT should be paid locally by the office receiving the shipment of goods, provided that such office has either (1) issued an invoice to the customer or (2) collected payment from the customer. Otherwise, VAT should be paid by the headquarters on a consolidated basis.

FIEs that wish to expand across China while optimizing EIT, BT, and VAT should evaluate the options offered by branches. Practice with respect to the tax treatment of branches varies substantially, and officials within the same tax bureau may take different views on certain issues, such as whether a branch company providing research services to its head office must pay BT. Through comprehensive planning and consulting with local tax officials, FIEs may be able to replicate advantages of tax structures with branches when expanding across China.

In principle, a branch registered in China may take the form of either an independent accounting branch, or a nonindependent accounting branch. Independent accounting branches are required to keep separate accounting records, which will have EIT consequences.

Some officials have indicated that they will permit a branch to operate as an independent accounting branch, and pay EIT to the local tax authorities, rather than to the authorities at the location of the FIE headquarters. This practice could be used to justify allocation of profits and losses among branches in multiple jurisdictions for purposes of minimizing EIT.

Comparison Between the Types of Entities

Table 12.1 lists the substantial differences between RO, an independent, and a non-independent accounting branch company.

Subsidiary and FICE

When an enterprise plans to expand its business by establishing "antennas" across areas, it may consider setting up a branch company. Such an entity structure may minimize the costs by offsetting the obligations of the parent company with the losses of the branches incurred. When the business develops further with greater revenues, the investor may establish the subsidiary company as the best choice. With that planning, the investor can benefit from the local tax policies.

Effective December 1, 2007, a new investment vehicle has been made available to foreign investors. The Chinese government encourages foreign investors to set up Foreign Investment Commercial Enterprises (FICEs) in China to conduct wholesale, retail, and other permitted business. Such types of business entities possess complete rights of trade and business. It can conduct import and export activities by itself, independent of local import and export companies, or by setting up a manufacturing company.

The FICE is a limited liability company wholly owned by the foreign investor, and it has total liberty to conduct trading, importing, and export activities. This has encouraged many different foreign investors to set up a FICE in one location, and expand rapidly by setting up branch companies of the FICE (see Chapter 2 on details of FICEs).

TABLE 12.1 Comparison Between the Types of Entities

	Representative Office	Independent Branch Company	Nonindependent Branch Company
Business Nature	Nonindependent legal entity	Nonindependent legal entity	Nonindependent legal entity
Invested Party	Foreign Companies	Foreign Invested Enterprises	Foreign Invested Enterprises
Capital Requirement	No	No	No
Accounting	Monthly Expense Report	Keep separate accounting records	No separate accounting records
Invoice	No right to issue invoices	Right to issue invoices	Cannot issue invoices
Sign Business Contract	No right to sign a business contract	If a contract is signed, the liability should be borne by the headquarters.	If a contract is signed, the liability should be borne by the headquarters.
Employment	No right to hire local staff independently; may employ through a qualified HR agency	Allowed to own employment rights, and the employment contract will be entered into between the branch company and the staff. The staff sign the employment contract with the FIE.	The staff sign the employment contract with the FIE.
Existing Term	The existing term of RO is no longer than three years, and can be renewed after certificates expire.	Restricted within the business term of the parent company	Restricted within the business term of the parent company
Establishment Condition	The RO is limited to register in an office building with foreign rental permission.	No location restrictions	No location restrictions

13

Mergers and Acquisitions in China

In recent years, we have witnessed the rapid development of mergers and acquisitions. Most corporate CFOs today will inevitably be required to be involved in mergers and acquisitions (M&A) involving China. In fact, it is commonly adopted as a strategic entry means into China's market. China, as one of the fastest-growing economies, with a huge domestic market, has seen a 400 percent increase in M&A activities in the past five years.

In this chapter, we will discuss some of the most important aspects of M&A activities in China as a guide for CFOs. First, we will review the M&A industry in China since the start of economic reforms in the last 30 years. Then, we will discuss how the economy has encouraged M&A activities, and how more and more companies have shifted from the traditional joint venture business strategy to more aggressive M&As. We will also discuss aspects of governmental policies and regulatory changes that will influence M&A activities in the next five to 10 years. Next, we will analyse a number of different scenarios that are happening in China:

- M&A of Chinese Domestic Companies
- M&A of Foreign Companies with Chinese companies
- M&A of Foreign Companies with foreign companies in China
- M&A of Chinese Companies with foreign companies in China and overseas

As a guide for CFOs, this chapter will discuss the importance of the accounting and financial aspects during the M&A process, and the importance of performing the proper due diligence and investigation of accounts. We will share a number of real-life cases.

As M&A is a massive topic in itself, there are a great number of laws and regulations governing it. We cannot attempt to cover such a large number of regulations. However, we will highlight the recent PRC rules and regulations regarding M&A activities, especially when they involve foreign players.

M&A in China

M&A is not a new term in the global marketplace. Goldman Sachs had already been involved in more than 100 deals in the late 1960s.[1] China also witnessed a number of M&As by foreign investors in the 1980s. However, these players were merely scratching the surface. In the 1990s, more M&A players came from all around the world to China. At the time, China viewed these foreign joint venture partners and newcomers from a protectionist point of view, and was mostly concerned with the impact these deals might have on its ongoing domestic economic and political reforms. Ever since China joined the World Trade Organization at the end of 2001, however, the Chinese government has opened up the market to foreign investors through deregulation and policy changes. At the beginning of the China economic reform 30 years ago, foreign direct investments (FDI) entered China mainly in the form of Greenfield investments. In the last few years, however, M&A has been on the rise. The American Chamber of Commerce in China has undertaken a survey among its members. More than 80 percent of the respondents cited a desire to serve customers in China and elsewhere in Asia as their reason for having a presence in China. This has an impact on the choice of using M&A as an easier tool to gain entry into China.

The Growth of M&As in China

The value of China's cross-border M&As by foreign investors was US$ 2.25 billion in 2002, accounting for 5.5 percent of its annual foreign direct investment (FDI). The percentage increased significantly in

2004 and 2005 to 11.16 percent and 13.68 percent, with M&A values topping US$ 6.67 billion and US$ 8.25 billion respectively. The M&A frenzy continued to gain momentum in 2006, with around 1,300 transactions approved by Chinese authorities. It is expected that the tide will keep rising at a rate of 25 to 30 percent for the next several years.

There are a number of reasons for the rapid increase in M&A activities in China. Besides deregulation and the liberalization of the capital markets, one of the most important reasons is the attractiveness of China's huge domestic market. Moreover, the market and various market segments are developing and growing rapidly. Strategic investors see M&A opportunities as an efficient way to gain bigger market share. Privatization and the restructuring of State Owned Enterprises (SOEs) also provide opportunities for foreign investors to access China's nationwide distribution networks. In the last 10 years, and even more so in the years ahead, Chinese domestic private companies will continue to seek international market expansion, and acquire advanced technology through M&A of overseas companies. Two years ago, Chinese domestic companies even went aboard to acquire foreign business.

With China opening up further in accordance with its WTO commitments, the finance, real estate, and infrastructure sectors will be the next potential fields for M&A activities. The Chinese government is encouraging SOEs in a few industrial sectors to consolidate into large integrated conglomerates, and to become global leaders in their own right.

Forms of M&A in China

Chinese Domestic Companies M&A

According to the *Financial Times*, the value of domestic M&A deals in China, including those in Hong Kong and Macau, in 2007 was up 53 percent from 2006 to US$ 50.6 billion.[2] The volume of deals grew 45 percent to 987 transactions, twice as much as foreign-invested M&A deals.

In China, mergers and acquisitions involve numerous government bodies. In particular, government bodies play the role of a regulator in each transaction. Apart from the supervision of antitrust and competition, regulations in industry sectors, as well as in approving authorities by the governments' bodies, transcend the general economic boundaries. Government participation includes review and even approval of the specific terms and conditions in the deal, in order to ensure the local economy's steady growth.

The Lenovo Story

A China-based computer company, Lenovo, made the first multi-international acquisition of IBM's PC division, marking the birth of the third-largest PC enterprise in the world. Lenovo, formerly known as Legend, is the largest PC manufacturer in China. The company was founded in 1984 as a distributor of IT products. Over the years, it has started its own PC business, growing to take the number one spot in China. Lenovo has paid US$ 1.25 billion for the whole PC business of IBM, including US$ 650 million in cash, and Lenovo shares valued at US$ 600 million. After the acquisition deal, Lenovo's PC business was expected to have an annual income of US$ 13 billion, with annual sales of about 14 million PCs.[*] Lenovo has a strong client base and sales infrastructure in the Chinese market, while IBM has a comprehensive network in PC sales on a global basis. The joint venture allows IBM to sell more services in China, while giving Lenovo the opportunity it has always craved for to expand beyond China.

[*] Michael Kanel los, "IBM Sells PC Group to Lenovo."
CNet News, December 8, 2004.

Foreign Companies' Acquisition of Chinese Companies

China's participation in the WTO and its open-door policies have allowed foreign investors to strategically enter Chinese markets under governmental supervision and support. The continuous trend of entries by foreign companies has met with different reactions from local Chinese companies. Multinationals are seeking M&As with local firms to take advantage of a lower manufacturing cost base, rapid market entry, a huge local market with established brands, as well as developed sales and sourcing networks. Out of all these factors, the greatest advantage of acquiring a Chinese company is speed. Foreign companies are well aware that they need several years and great efforts to obtain local market share, loyal customers, sales points, human resources, and so forth.

Domestic Bliss

The First Automobile Works (FAW) merger with Tianjin Automotive Xiali (TAIC) eventually came through following joint negotiations between the government and the enterprises.* The two Chinese major economy-car producers received government approval for the transfer of a controlling stake in TAIC to FAW. Both companies were involved in economy-car production, and this joint venture is the biggest ever asset regrouping between national auto companies in China. The deal enables FAW, a state-owned firm with assets worth RMB 59 billion, to move into small-car production. This deal also made Japanese car producer Toyota a cooperative partner of FAW, making the latter the biggest shareholder in a joint venture between TAIC and Toyota. This merger also enables the two groups to step up restructuring, expand their business scope, and improve their market competitiveness. It is a win-win situation for both to meet the challenges arising from China's entry into the World Trade Organization (WTO). The government has showed itself to be supportive of such domestic deals.

* "FAW Wins China Approval for Purchase of Tianjin Automotive." *Autoparts Report*, September 16, 2002.

The acquisition of Chinese target companies by foreign companies has not always been smooth sailing over the years. The Chinese government has promulgated laws and regulations to govern these acquisitions. The latest is Order No. 10 (Rules on Acquisition and Merger of Domestic Enterprises by Foreign Investors). Prior to this promulgation, in the year 2003, there was an earlier set of Provisional M&A Rules, which has been suspended. In the latest promulgation, one of the key regulations is the Anti-Monopoly Law that restricts strategic investors from obtaining a substantial market share. Such a regulation has created obstacles for some companies that are trying to acquire local Chinese companies.

> ## MRA to JV
>
> A U.S. private equity firm, the Carlyle Group, paid RMB 1.22 billion (US$ 154 million) for a 45 percent stake in Xugong Construction Machinery,* China's biggest construction machinery maker, an industry leader that owns several advanced technologies. China's Ministry of Commerce was concerned that foreign control of key Chinese firms could threaten the country's economic security. The deal eventually turned from a pure M&A into a joint venture with an investment of RMB 4.2 billion and registered capital of nearly RMB 1.5 billion.
>
> *Laura Santini, "Carlyle Group to Acquire 85% of Chinese Construction Firm." *Wall Street Journal*, October 25, 2005.

Government Involvement

Challenges may arise with governmental involvement. In most cases, the merger structure, the type of target, the transaction value, and the nature of investment all come into consideration in negotiations between governments and foreign investors. After 20 years' development, China's policies and concerns have shifted into supporting high-tech and environmentally friendly industries, which were not evident concerns in the 1980s and 1990s.

China is generally known to have become more receptive to foreign investors' cross-border M&A deals in the last three to five years. Many multinational companies today, particularly foreign companies and private equity funds prefer to acquire local players directly. Especially for private equity, the deals that are being closed are getting larger. There were 11 deals of over US$ 100 million in the first six months of 2007 compared to only one in 2006.

Private Equity Groups and Strategic Investors

Private equity groups and strategic investors also have been playing a role in a variety of scenarios. The value of private equity investments has almost doubled from US$ 5.7 billion in 2006 to almost US$

11 billion in 2007. In the United States, private equity groups tend to purchase controlling or majority interests in companies, but in China, opportunities to purchase a controlling interest are rare. Chinese entrepreneurs use a family business model. They may not trust foreign investors, especially foreign investors who are insistent on getting control. As a result, private equity funds in China tend to operate as late-stage venture capital investors, and they are active in technology industries such as healthcare, agriculture, pharmaceuticals, and energy. More home-grown private equity firms are emerging in the domestic market due to the recently permitted "limited partnership" entities, which have created more favorable conditions for the formation of domestic private equity funds. Such domestic private equity also has the convenience of raising RMB-denominated funds.

Foreign Companies Acquiring Foreign Companies in China

Some cases of M&A deals have taken place in China because players found themselves in competition with one another. Often, foreign investors find it necessary to join forces with each other purely because China is just too large geographically to handle alone, in addition to the challenges posed by cultural differences.

Chinese Companies acquiring Foreign Companies in China and Overseas

In the first 11 months of 2007, the value of deals in which Chinese companies acquired shares of companies in other countries more than doubled to US$ 16.4 billion as the country's global ambitions grew. However, most of these Chinese companies own only minority stakes in the foreign companies.

Such activities have been even more aggressive in the banking industry. Industrial and Commercial Bank of China, has taken a 20 percent stake in Standard Bank in South Africa.

Most of the initiatives in acquiring overseas companies have been led by the Chinese government. Over the last 30 years of economic reform and aggressive export trade, the Chinese government has built large foreign reserves, amounting to US$ 1.5 trillion in 2007. At the same time, there is a continual need to use these revenues prudently, which led to the formation of the China Investment Corporation

---

Ladies Only

L'Oréal, a leading French women's cosmetics maker, purchased the Chinese women's cosmetics brand, Yue-Sai* (founded by a Chinese-American) in 2004. This was partially because the Yue-Sai brand was user-friendly, and its style of beauty was much more appealing to Chinese customers. Yue-Sai, founded in 1992, had been owned by a French cosmetics company Coty since 1996. Yue-Sai is a major brand with a strong market position, and is sold in 240 cities in China. L'Oréal has been operating in the Chinese market since 1997, and has a substantial market share, along with other foreign brands like Lancôme and Maybelline. L'Oréal targeted Yue-Sai because it has many loyal Chinese consumers. As part of the deal, L'Oréal acquired a manufacturing plant in Shanghai, which it plans to use to boost the production capacity of its brands for the Asian market. Furthermore, a brand like Yue-Sai, is symbolic for today's Chinese women. This acquisition fits naturally into L'Oréal's portfolio. The move also suggests a period of brand consolidation for the fragmented industry, with many manufacturers. This acquisition has strengthened the group's leadership in the makeup and facial skin-care industry.

*Paul Denlinger, "L'Oréal Buys Local Chinese Cosmetics Brand Yue-Sai." *China Business Strategy,* January 2, 2005.

(CIC) in May 2007, with assets of US$ 200 billion. The CIC has since invested in Blackstone, the world's top private equity firm.

Chinese companies' acquisition of foreign companies is relatively new. Many Chinese companies still lack experience or expertise in these areas, and they rely greatly on business partners.

Corporate CFOs Need to Know China M&A Regulations

China has a very different business culture from other countries in the world. To become familiar with this business culture is already a very difficult task, let alone to carry out a successful M&A in China. Foreign

---

Peace Offer

In late 2007, Ping An Insurance, the country's second-largest life insurer, took a 4.2 percent stake in a European banking and insurance group.* On November 27, Ping An bought 95.01 million Fortis shares on the Euronext Brussels and Euronext Amsterdam for US$ 2.69 billion. The domestic insurance company founded in 1988 was the first insurance company in China, and the first nationwide insurance company to receive strategic investment from overseas companies. The acquisition targets Fortis as it was an international provider of banking and insurance services to personal, business, and institutional customers. The acquisition of a 4.2 percent stake sets a precedent for cross-border alliances. Ping An will benefit from Fortis's expertise in cross-selling, risk management, and product design on the global stage. This is an incredible benefit beyond financial returns for Ping An. Meanwhile, this investment has allowed Fortis to gain enhanced access to high-growth markets, particularly in China.

*Kay Murchie, "Ping An Insurance Buys Stake in Fortis."
All Financial News, December 3, 2007.

---

corporate CFOs who become involved in M&A activities in China must develop a good grasp of the different M&A regulations there.

Order No. 10

Effective from September 8. 2006, Order No. 10, "Rules on Acquisition and Merger of Domestic Enterprises by Foreign Investors," was jointly issued by six PRC government agencies. The Order aims to improve the M&A regulatory environment and encourage outbound investments by domestic enterprises. It also aims to strengthen the protection of China's key assets and companies (whether state-owned or privately owned) from being acquired by foreign investors. The three key aspects covered in the Order are as follows:

Quasi-FIEs, specifically defined in the Order, are domestic enterprises that acquire their own shares through the creation of offshore

Learning from Experience

CNOOC announced its intention to place a cash bid for Uncoal at US\$ 67 per share, totaling US\$ 18.5 billion.[*] Two months later, the China National Offshore Oil Company Ltd. (CNOOC) withdrew its bid for Unocal when it did not increase its earlier bid to challenge Chevron's bid to take over the California-based oil company. As one of the largest state-owned oil giants in China, CNOOC is exclusively engaged in oil and gas with a competitive core business along the value chain. In recent years, through a series of reforms and asset acquisitions, CNOOC has experienced a great leap forward and has strengthened its image. The bid met with unexpected political opposition in U.S. political circles, where certain people viewed the proposed merger as a threat to America, citing security threats including the possible transfer of military technology to China. Political pressure was one of the major reasons that CNOOC withdrew the offer. Although the acquisition was not successful, it was still a good experience for Chinese companies, many of which are adopting a so-called going-out strategy and seeking global expansion.

[*]Brian Turner, "CNOOC Abandons Unocal Bid."
All Financial News, August 2, 2005.

special-purpose vehicles (SPVs). The Order excludes them from being classified as FIEs. When an offshore SPV acquires a related domestic enterprise, thereby converting it to an FIE, the M&A activity must be approved by the Ministry of Commerce (MOFCOM).

Special-Purpose Vehicles Share Swaps

Cross-border share swaps can be utilized as a form of payment. The regulatory framework of a cross-border share swap by a public company as a form of payment is set out by the Order for the first time in PRC regulations. The basic requirements, application procedures, and special rules for offshore SPVs have been covered in the Order. In particular, domestic enterprises are required to engage a professional

M&A advisor who is registered in China to perform the due diligence review required of the foreign investor.

Antimonopoly Rules and National Security Concerns

Antimonopoly issues are also addressed in the Order as it emphasizes the importance of certain key state economic interests. The relevant transaction parties are required to report to the MOFCOM if the M&A activity:

- Involves strategically important industries
- Has or may have impact on state economic security
- Causes a transfer of actual controlling rights of a domestic enterprise that owns well-known trademarks or Chinese traditional brand names

With a more mature platform to regulate M&A activities, there are positive indications that the legal environment for inbound M&A in China is becoming more flexible and transparent with detailed procedures and guidelines. It is exciting to see more foreign investors moving into China by strategic takeover and encountering new challenges. There are, at the same time, very important developments in other laws and regulations, such as income tax reform, new labor contract law, and so forth. Foreign M&A players must stay alert to these changes.

The Importance of Accounting in M&A

In an M&A transaction, the role of the accountant is very important in matters such as the valuation of the target company, the performance of the financial and tax due diligence of the company, and the financial structure of the deal. Our experience indicates that most of the M&A attempts in China will not pass the due diligence stage. One of the key reasons for the high failure rate is that the records for many aspects of Chinese companies are not readily available. Some Chinese companies have two or more sets of accounting books to manipulate financial data, either to exaggerate the company performance in order to borrow loans from financial institutions, or to minimize the company's performance for tax avoidance purposes. Of course, there are the accounting reports for management purposes, which represent the true picture of the company. Therefore, the whole process of a M&A transaction is more complicated from the target search and negotiations, to due diligence, accurate valuation, and post-deal integration.

Accounting in Different M&A Phases

Before the M&A Transaction

The preliminary phase in M&A is to identify the M&A objectives and develop the strategy. The objectives must be aligned with the organization's vision, both in the short and long term. When the objectives are laid out clearly the company then needs to seek a target company. Companies sometimes will engage professional advisors from the early stages of the M&A to assist in screening targets.

Valuation Approaches

Once a target company is identified and the initial M&A interest is expressed, certain financial information, such as previous annual book revenue, will become available. This information can be used for the estimation of the potential long-term revenue stream, payback, and other economic risk factors, which can be taken into account in the valuation process. There are a number of valuation approaches; the following three are commonly adopted in practice:

Discounted Cash Flow (DCF) Income Approach

This approach is calculated based on the after-tax cash flow discounted at a rate that is commensurate with the risk profile. The three elements taken into consideration are growth rate, discount rate, and terminal value. The DCF approach calculates the future earning potential, which is the key investment criterion. It also takes into account the time value of money.

Market Comparison Approach

This approach involves the comparison of different financial information with a selection of listed companies in the market, which are similar in size and in business. This financial information of the comparable companies provide good references for the valuations of the target. For example, Price over Earnings (P/E), Price over Revenues (P/R), Price over Net Worth (P/NW), Price over Earnings before Interest and Tax (P/EBIT), Price over Earnings before Interest, Tax, Depreciation, and Amortisation (P/EBITDA).

Net Assets Approach

This is usually used when the buyer is only buying the net assets of the target company. This method determines the value based on the balance sheet. It considers the value of the company as the aggregate value of the individual assets, less the aggregate value of the individual liabilities of the company. The valuation methods include net assets book value, net assets adjusted book value, and net assets liquidation value.

Due to the nature of the business culture in China, several difficulties may be encountered during valuation. Most Chinese target companies, especially their owners, do not appreciate Western accountants' methods of valuation. They always believe that their companies are worth a lot given the vastness of the Chinese market. Therefore many figures can be extrapolated to very big numbers. Over the years, this perception has somewhat changed, but very slowly. There are more Chinese entrepreneurs who are now beginning to appreciate how foreign buyers value their companies. In addition, ever-changing regulations continue to create difficulties in assessing market risks. The reliability of financial information is one of the biggest barriers, such as inappropriate capitalization of expenses, hidden costs, and insufficient provisions on inventories and receivables.

During the M&A Transaction

The role of financial professionals in the execution of an M&A transaction is to carry out the financial and tax due diligence. Due diligence is the process of investigation usually carried out by a neutral third party, for instance, an accounting firm, on behalf of a party contemplating a business transaction for the purpose of evaluating business risks.

Financial Due Diligence

Financial due diligence during the pre-bid phase involves a review of available information, identification of key issues, and providing a basis for the indicative valuation. Due diligence is usually performed after the valuation and before the transaction starts. There are three phases in due diligence, each of which is carried out with various levels of analysis of business risks in the different stages in M&A.

• *Initial Due Diligence.* The financial professionals will collect and perform an initial analysis on provided financial data and identify the business risks. Simple tasks may take up a lot of time during the initial due diligence in China, especially those pertaining to government and regulatory approvals to set up an entity in order to exercise M&A activity. Since M&A is relatively new to Chinese businessmen, some potential targets are often unwilling to cooperate and conduct a due diligence review before they are certain about the transaction. Furthermore, the financial statements may not be transparent, and may be questionable in terms of accuracy, due to differences in accounting policies: for instance, People's Republic of China General Accepted Accounting Procedures (PRC GAAP) versus the International Financial Reporting Standards (IFRS).

• *Detailed Due Diligence.* An in-depth due diligence includes site visits and interviews with key management to gather more information to be analyzed together with the information from the pre-M&A Phase. Usually, the financial statement analysis states the quality of earnings, the normalized income statement, the quality of assets, the off-balance-sheet assets, and the exposure of liabilities and commitments.

• *Final Due Diligence.* This is carried out at the end of an M&A transaction, and involves the performance of a final review when closing a deal. The objective is to double-confirm the business risks that are identified and the follow-up procedures.

Typical problems relating to PRC targets include the following:

• Multiple sets of accounting books
• Financial records that show high profitability, but with no cash in the bank
• High levels of related-party transactions
• High balance of account receivables
• Insufficient provision of employee social security contributions
• High levels of inventory holding
• Lots of high-level prepayments
• Other regulatory issues

Tax Due Diligence

The tax due diligence can be very critical in China due to the rapidly changing tax rules and regulations. The performance of tax due diligence by an accounting firm can provide insights to the tax exposures of the target company: that is, whether the company is tax compliant. The impact from the local Tax Authorities may be different, according to different cities and provinces. A tax due diligence can also change the M&A structure from an equity transaction to an asset transaction to avoid any contingent tax liabilities.

The tax due diligence should be carried out based on the major applicable taxes, which include corporate income tax, value added tax, business tax, consumption tax, individual income tax, land value added tax, stamp duties, and customs duties.

Issues Associated with Tax Compliance

There are number of common tax due diligence issues relating to PRC target companies. For example, there can be aggressive and unjustifiable tax schemes in which Chinese companies may have understated revenue or overstated expenses to minimize their tax liability. There can even be special deals with local authorities and unofficial tax concessions, although this is less common in the bigger cities. The foreign acquirer will also need to comply with its own relevant corrupt practice laws and regulations (the Foreign Corrupt Practice Act (FCPA) in the United States) and additional review may be needed in such circumstances. Tax due diligence is extremely important in such areas as corporate and individual tax compliance, as unsupported transfer pricing practices, may lead to heavy penalty exposures and late payment surcharges. The related party transactions in China may sometimes not be very transparent either. Tax due diligence will need to identify whether transactions are carried out at arm's length. The latest PRC Corporate Income Tax (CIT) has specifically outlined the regulations for transfer pricing.

Post-M&A Transactions

A successful M&A transaction is not based only on the value of the deal and the time spent on it. A good deal has been achieved when there is effective integration of the acquired company, and the M&A objectives are achieved. Therefore, post-M&A corporate matters and corporate secretarial works are crucial. There will be large numbers of documents to be filed, including incorporation of a new entity for M&A purposes, transfer of shares and assets, and liquidation of the target company. The average process in an M&A deal takes from 12 to 24 months in China, whereas the timing expectation in overseas deals is only 6 to 12 months.

The integration after M&A can also take a long time and become complicated. These integrations include finance and administration integration, human resources integration, information technology integration, corporate culture integration, and so forth.

China is famous for its ever-changing rules and regulations. Complying with all necessary documentations, in accordance with different government authorities, will require time and experience. Foreign CFOs must keep up to date with different requirements. Especially in M&A activities, the recent Order No. 10 has outlined the boundaries in which foreign investors can carry out M&A in China.

Other Recent Rules and Regulations

New M&A regulatory changes in 2006 are a reflection of the ongoing evolution of China's accounting, tax, and legal environment, as these regulations race to keep up with changes in the broader domestic and global economy. The changes introduced in 2006 reflect the fact that the government has now accepted M&A as a necessary tool in China's ongoing economic development. This is important because it allows fragmented industries to consolidate and grow from local and regional bases to become nationally and internationally competitive. Another noteworthy regulatory reform, although it does not directly impact M&A, is the new corporate income tax law (CIT) that has been effective since January 1, 2008. This law unified the two separate corporate income tax regimes that were applied to domestic and foreign companies, eliminating the preferences enjoyed by foreign investors, while at the same time lowering the maximum tax rate from 33 percent to 25 percent.

Conclusion

Since China's economic growth has been phenomenal, there will be more incentives for strategic investors from all around the world to establish their share of the market via many paths, including M&A.

The overall state of economic growth facilitates an active M&A market as companies look to restructure, grow in scale, and develop new markets. As foreign companies continue to be active in the market, domestic M&As will continue due to government support and restructuring of state-owned enterprises (SOEs). Stronger domestic companies will make plans for expansion in the global market. CFOs will be required to keep up to date with ever-changing rules and regulations, to take control throughout the process.

Endnotes

1. Jonathan Knee, *The Accidental Investment Banker: Inside the Decade that Transformed Wall Street.* New York: Oxford University Press, 2006.
2. Justin Lau, "Domestic deals power surge in Chinese M&A." *Financial Times*, December 18, 2007.

14

Financing Options

F oreign investors who enter the Chinese market are usually capitalized and financed by their parent companies. These arrangements
are common because as foreigners in China, they may not venture into
other options in an alien land. Moreover Foreign investments in China
have to start as "foreign direct investments" (FDIs). Therefore, the
Chinese government expects the initial capital to be funded directly by
the parent company.

In this chapter, we will restrict our discussion to how a foreign
invested enterprise (FIE) can seek other options of financing in China
after its initial set-up period. We will not deal with financing options
that are available to domestic companies, because these issues are far
more complex. In any case, the discussion here will not be exhaustive,
since the banking and financial institution industry in China is ever so
fluid and is going through various changes. Therefore, the modes and
options will also change very fast. This is in line with China's commitment to the WTO, wherein the financial services industry was eventually opened up at the end of 2006.

Financing by Parent Company
for Initial Capital Purposes

As discussed above, a foreign investor has to inject capital when it sets
up a subsidiary in China. Earlier chapters discussed registered capital
and the capital verification process. These still apply in today's context.

Letters of Credit

Over the years, foreign bankers who are familiar with their foreign corporate clients (and vice versa) have developed various other financial tools, or options for their clients. Some foreign banks have been issuing stand-by letters of credit (SBLC) outside China to fund parent companies with their initial capital requirements when they need it to set up their subsidiaries. Traditionally, such letters of credit or LCs are used to finance the company's working capital requirements. However, given the constraints of China's requirements, such short-term SBLCs are used to mezzanine long-term capital requirements.

In the actual process, the banker will issue SBLCs that allow the parent company to draw down working capital. Such working capital would be used for capital injection into the subsidiaries. In turn, the subsidiaries are able to purchase goods from the parent company. They would in turn repay the parent companies for the goods purchased.

This mechanism is currently available and widely used by foreign financial institutions and banks.

Obviously, if an investor company has its own cash for long-term investment purposes, it will still be better off to utilize such internal resources for investment into its subsidiaries. Many foreign multinationals prefer to adopt this method instead of having to deal with their bankers, especially if the capital injection amount is not significant.

Phasing Out Capital Injections

According to China's foreign investment regulations, foreign investors are allowed to make capital injections in stages over a period of time: for example, a foreign trading WFOE can have its parent company inject the first 20 percent of the registered capital within three months of obtaining its temporary business licenses. The balance of the 80 percent can be injected within the next two years. For manufacturing companies, the period allowed can be even longer. The CFO needs to consider not just what is allowed, but also the true needs of the business operations.

Banking Relationships

Most foreign companies, especially the smaller and medium companies, may also require short-term financing for their businesses in China in the initial phase at setting up. Since they are more familiar with their bankers at home, they will naturally seek help from them. In such a context, it is important to find out from bankers in home countries if they operate branches in China. Most of the foreign banks consider Shanghai as a key financial center, and therefore likely to have a presence there. Foreign banks that do not have a presence in Shanghai, Beijing, or other Tier One cities, may have corresponding interbanking relationships with local Chinese banks. Such relationships, if well established, allow foreign companies to tap into the network of the local domestic banks.

The Big Five Chinese Banks

If a foreign business cannot utilize its own bank (with a presence in China), it must find a domestic bank in China. Traditionally the banking industry has been dominated by the Big Five:

- Bank of China (BOC): Traditionally, BOC takes care of international trade when China deals with the outside world.
- Agriculture Bank: Traditionally, this bank is responsible for financing the agricultural industry and farmers.
- Industrial and Commercial Banking Corporation (ICBC): Traditionally, this bank is responsible for financing commerce and industry.
- China Construction Bank (CCB): This bank is traditionally responsible for financing the construction industry.
- Bank of Communications: This bank is traditionally responsible for financing major communications and transportation projects.

Ever since the opening up of China, the responsibilities of these Big Five banks have been somewhat liberalized, and they are no longer restricted in scope. However, by virtue of history and traditions, each of these banks still has exceptional strengths in its traditional areas.

Other Banks

In the last 30 years, China has also seen the growth and development of other big banks. They include Citic Bank, China Merchant Bank, Minsheng Bank, and other Tier Two banks. Being fairly new, these banks do not have the burden (包袱) of the Big Five banks, which have to keep many staff employed to fulfil social responsibilities. They are also more exposed to international practices. In terms of service quality, they learn faster from the international banks that have ventured into China, both at the corporate and individual level. They are also offering more products and services.

Short-Term Financing

Short-term financing is critical not only for establishing the company, but also for small and medium businesses. Most banks, both Chinese domestic banks and foreign banks, offer some form of short-term financing, normally for a period of less than two years. Typically, these banks offer trade-credit financing. This normally takes the form of letters of credit that extend over various numbers of days, for example, LC 60, LC 90, and LC 180. These credit facilities are commonly offered to manufacturing companies when they need to purchase raw materials, either in China or from overseas suppliers. They are also offered to trading companies.

However, the bankers, both local and foreign, can be very stringent. Some form of collateral or securities on mortgages is required. It is very seldom that a local Chinese bank will offer such credit without something in return. Very recently, foreign banks may be willing to lend on a more "open" basis; they may not necessarily require collateral, but rather some form of guarantee of repayment from the parent company. Certain foreign banks are more sophisticated in offering tailor-made solutions for domestic and cross-boarder trade. This sophistication comes from the ability to measure payment risk for each transaction.

Mid- to Long-Term Financing

For the small and mid-size company in China, the first or second year is the most critical in determining whether the company will survive in the Chinese market. Some businesses may not be able to endure even the initial six to eight months.

If foreign businesses can weather the first year and stabilize their business, they can then plan ahead for their finances on a medium- to long-term basis, and begin to look at medium- to long-term financing options. Here are some of the medium- to long-term financing options that maybe available to foreign businesses.

Increase in Registered Capital

If the business is confident in the medium term, most foreign subsidiaries can request the parent company to finance the operation. This is, by far, the most common mode of increase in finance, especially if the increase is not huge. Most parent companies will not want their Chinese subsidiaries to be laden with debt, so they may be willing to finance the subsidiaries. Chapter 2 discussed Registered Capital (RC) and Total Investment (TI). The increase in the RC is restricted by the amount of TI. There are detailed processes to be adhered when increasing the RC (see Chapter 2).

Loans from Shareholders

Some parent companies, although confident of the performance of their Chinese subsidiaries, may not wish to pump in additional capital in the form of RC or equity increase. They may also want the subsidiaries to observe discipline in cash and capital utilization, and so they may be willing to extend the shareholders' loan to the subsidiaries over the medium to long term, for example three to five years. In such situations, the parent company can determine and expect repayment from the subsidiaries. The subsidiaries are also expected to pay interest if the loan is set up that way. Such loan repayments also mean returns will come in at different points in time, rather than just with the year-end dividend.

They are several strict procedures and processes to adhere to when a parent company (from abroad) extends such foreign currency loans to its subsidiaries in China. (see Chapter 4 on the details of shareholders' loans.) Many companies commit mistakes by not adhering to such processes and procedures. For instance, they may simply remit foreign currency as advances to their subsidiaries, not realizing that the subsidiaries may not be able to pay these sums back. So, it is important to abide by these procedures if proper shareholder loan financing is to be extended to subsidiaries.

Mid- to Long-Term Bank Financing

For many foreign manufacturing companies in China, who are often more heavily capitalized than service or trading companies, such medium- to long-term financing options may not be readily available from their parent companies. Due to the regulations and restrictions on bank lending, most banks will require some form of collateral or mortgage for medium- to long-term loans. Manufacturing companies may mortgage land, properties, or equipment in order to secure financing. It is very common for domestic Chinese banks to access the value of assets being pledged as securities. Besides accessing the value of the assets, banks will also look at the business model, creditworthiness, and cash flow situation of the company. Foreign banks that have received a referral or introduction from their own parent banks will be more comfortable with the company.

When they lend to companies, both local Chinese and foreign banks can operate in Renminbi (RMB) and foreign currency. If the company borrows in RMB, it avoids the risks of exchange fluctuation. Hence if the company earns RMB revenue, borrows in RMB from the banks, and repays in RMB, the currencies will be aligned. This is a significant difference as compared to the shareholders' loans, which occur only in foreign currencies.

Leasing

In the last two years, China has opened up the financial services industry to foreign financial institutions. Multinational and mid-size leasing companies have been opening shops in Tier One cities such as Shanghai and Beijing. Leasing companies can operate traditional finance leases and operating leases for companies. Typically, leasing companies are very willing to arrange equipment and vehicle financing. Although the interest cost may be slightly higher than with traditional banks, leasing as an alternative is becoming more widely used, especially by foreign companies operating in China. The leasing mechanism is also spreading to traditional Chinese companies, although traditional Chinese companies are geared more toward buying outright than toward leasing. However, foreign leasing companies are now able to factor in risk considerations, and structure the leasing deal with more sophistication, and on more reasonable terms. We will see an increase in such leasing.

Conclusion

This discussion is a guide for small-to-medium investors on the financing options that they can use for their operations in China. However, banks and financial institutions will be able to offer more sophisticated products and services. CFOs should also conduct detailed evaluations of the financing options with their bankers.

15

Negotiation

M any stories that have spread across business circles claim that the Chinese are tough people to deal with, especially in negotiations. Earlier chapters have covered issues that related to such negotiations. Chapters 1, 2 and 15 are especially relevant.

Negotiation is an art. Negotiations can be especially complex in China as a result of 30 years of rapid economic reform. This chapter discusses some specific aspects of what a CFO may face in negotiations.

Negotiating in China

Negotiation is usually considered to be a compromise in which we try to settle an argument or issue to benefit ourselves as much as possible. Communication is always the key in negotiation, whether face-to-face, on the telephone, or in writing.

Trading in China is a great challenge. Negotiating with the Chinese is an even more complicated affair for Western companies. Negotiation is constant, starting from the establishment of a business and continuing into its day-to-day activities. Negotiation in China is one of the most frequently cited reasons for the failure of many foreign enterprises.

CFOs nowadays are not only expected to have technical skills, but also interpersonal skills. How can a foreign CFO overcome these difficulties in negotiations? What are the techniques required to negotiate in China? We will discuss the major categories of people that foreign CFOs have to deal with when they are doing business in China. We will highlight the important things to be aware of when the CFO negotiates with each category. We will also provide some in-depth social cultural understanding of Chinese negotiation processes, and discuss resources where CFOs can seek assistance.

Government Bodies

Due to China's sheer size, the multiple layers of government structures and bureaucracy are extremely complex. The requirements of each government body may vary. Each of the government bodies may interpret, and hence, enforce regulations differently. Therefore, CFOs must learn to deal with these ever-changing interpretations. The major government bodies CFOs will frequently come across are the Tax Authorities (税务局), the State Administration for Industry and Commerce (SAIC, 工商局), the State Administration of Foreign Exchange (SAFE, 外汇管理局), and the Municipal Labour Bureau (人事劳动局), just to mention only a few.

The Tax Authority

The Tax Authority is a major government body that any company has to deal with on a regular basis. As discussed in the earlier chapters, there are a number of different offices under the Tax Authority. Each company has a dedicated tax officer from the Tax Authority, who will be the main communicator between the company's accountants and the Tax Authority. The tax officer will oversee the tax compliance of the company, according to his or her interpretation of the tax law. In this instance, "communication" (沟通) may be a more appropriate word than "negotiation." However, there are certain techniques that improve communication with the tax officer. Language may be essential. Although there are many foreign companies in Tier One cities like Beijing, Shanghai, and Shenzhen, these tax officers are not likely to speak English. In addition to the language barriers, the accountant who is in communication with the tax officer must have a strong understanding of the company's business activities, and extensive technical knowledge of the rules and regulations.

This knowledge will empower the accountant to face the challenges from the tax officers. In one case, a company had missed its monthly tax filing submission date by two days when it was first established, although the tax filing would have been nil. The tax officer could charge a fine on the company for late payment. An experienced accountant, however, might be able to negotiate with the tax officer to have the fine waived.

Baijiu Diplomacy

The company was supposed to be awarded the "five-year tax exemption and five-year half-tax" incentive (五免五减) since its investment exceeded RMB 1 billion. Despite much effort by the CFO, however, the Municipal Tax Authority was not very proactive about carrying through with the process to award the certificate to the company. Subsequently, a new CFO took over. He understood the mindset of the Tax Chief, who would be hindering the process. The Tax Chief wanted the company to come forward to build the relationship over the long term. In any event, the billion-dollar investment company is a player. The new CFO decided to have dinner with the Tax Chief (after several requests) and his officers. It was just a simple dinner. However, the tax people were able to come to an understanding with the foreign CFO, and vice versa. Coming from a foreign country, the CFO had to "endure" the extremely alcoholic Chinese white liquor (白酒) throughout the dinner. However, the tax people could feel the sincerity of the new CFO. Three months later, the company was awarded the certificate.

These case studies have highlighted that the Tax Authority is a body that accountants and CFOs will have to face constantly. To achieve their objectives, CFOs must understand the mindset and perceptions of these officials. In Chinese, as expressed in the *Thirty-Six Strategies of Sun Tzu* (孙子兵法三十六计), this is known as "knowing yourself and knowing your opponent" (知己知彼).

In Detail

A Singapore-based company specialising in thin film deposition and semiconductor packaging applications identified China as the next key growth market, and decided to set up a sales and manufacturing facility in Suzhou. The company approached the Investment Bureau, and was advised that equipment being invested would be exempted from import VAT. However, when the application was filed with the Customs, it was rejected. The company approached a consulting firm, and the next morning, the consultants were there to rectify the original application rejected by the Customs. With the help of the consultants in communication and negotiations, the Customs advised the company to amend the description of the equipment and address the requirements more specifically. The consultants further facilitated the meeting of the Customs higher authorities with the client. In this way, they were able to help the company to push through their application, and achieved approximately US$ 90,000 in cost savings.

Negotiations with Customers and Suppliers

A CFO doing business in China will be required to engage in negotiations with suppliers and customers. It is important to have clear contracts with them. Although many will say that paper contracts are less useful than *guanxi*, in reality, they are essential in doing business in China. The contracts must clearly state the exact terms of payment, performance standards, and timelines. They require full attention to details, such as initialing pages of contracts, and proper signing. Professionals such as accountants, lawyers, and bankers will be able to provide valuable advice on common practices, as well as the best safeguards for a foreign business. One key point in a contract with clients and customers is payment terms. It is common business practice in China for customers to drag out their payments. The CFO needs to be strict about this. Payment terms should be executed by using letters of credit, or requiring customers to make advance payment, such as a 50 percent down payment.

The contract should also state the payment currencies: for example, whether you want to be paid in U.S. dollars or RMB. You should be certain that the currency is what you want upon receipt. If your customers want to pay in U.S. dollars while you are paying your suppliers in Renminbi, with the continually depreciating U.S. dollar, you may want to negotiate with your customers to protect the loss in foreign exchange. There are many foreign banks and advisors in China to propose the most appropriate financial instruments to protect converted currencies.

Understand the Culture Before the Negotiations Begin

Business negotiations in China can be very frustrating for Western business people. Compared to the direct and straightforward negotiation style of the West, Chinese tend to be more indirect and conservative. This can be time consuming. However, it is important to follow these unwritten rules. Patience is key in Chinese business negotiations. The Chinese culture sometimes makes people suspicious of strangers. The initial meeting could be just an introductory session. It is very likely that no productive decision will be made at the initial meetings. However, it is important to make the Chinese party feel comfortable with you. Interpersonal skills are required here to establish good relationships so things can go smoothly after.

Understanding the hierarchy and identifying the decision maker in the negotiation process is also helpful. Hierarchy is a huge issue in Chinese business settings. It determines who enters a meeting room first, how introductions are made, how seating is arranged in meetings and at dinner, who speaks, and who makes decisions. In China, the emphasis is on equality of counterparts. For example, it is common practice for a director-level executive to meet a director-level counterpart to show sincerity, through status equality, as well as the importance that is attached to the relationship. For example, it will be good for the CFO, or even the CEO, to meet with the Tax Chief, or Deputy Tax Chief in a meeting to discuss matters.

Seeking Expert Assistance

There are no shortcuts. Everything is a learning process. Utilizing informal professional networks and their expertise to help you in negotiations can be crucial. These local professionals not only provide business and cultural insights, but also have *guanxi* in many respects. The panel of experts should be a combination of public accountants, lawyers, human resources advisors or recruiters, and translators. These specialists can provide you with the most updated information about regulations to increase your negotiating power, so that you know what you are negotiating for. For example, accountants can advise you on changes in the VAT refund rate, and a CFO can use this information to negotiate with exporters from overseas. A skillful lawyer can draw up a contract that will prevent many problems. A good HR agency can assist you to negotiate better when you are hiring local employees. They can advise you on benchmark salaries and benefits packages. You may feel powerless when you are negotiating in a different country with a completely different language and culture. A good translator should not only overcome language barriers, but also understand appropriate negotiation techniques. It is valuable to have all these professionals (accountants, lawyers, and HR agencies) to be able to speak the same language as you

Furthermore, these specialists should not be just information providers, but also be value added service providers who can offer advice and recommendations. The public accountant could be in a very powerful position when it comes to negotiating with the tax authorities.

Have a Contingency Plan

There are no guaranteed results in China. It is always good to have backup plans for each stage of a process to ensure the pace of progress. Due to China's ever-changing rules and regulations, and its diversified culture and people, it is important to identify risks and have a more conventional negotiation theory. Assessing your escape strategy is useful in stable situations, but less helpful in a changing environment. Searching for problems before they materialize is crucial. Creating scenarios of what can go wrong, and strategies to deal with potential problems is wise, so too are knowing the limits on losses, and setting milestones for performance.

16

Culture

In discussions about doing business in any foreign place, the cultural aspects of the country always come up. Even in today's world where globalization and technology seem to prevail, it would be wrong to ignore how much cultural behavior can affect business. When it comes to the historic richness, traditional practices and beliefs, sheer geographical size, and the number of ethnic groups, China is second to none. All of these add to the complexity of integrating culture with business.

History

China's 5,000 years of history are rich in every sense of the word. It is a very refined culture. This chapter will not explore Chinese culture in detail. This would be impossible in one book, or even a series of books. We will simply share a few experiences of how Chinese culture can affect foreign businesses, enough to give CFOs and other business people some sense of the culture.

From the Xia Dynasty (夏朝) beginning around 2000 B.C. through the Qin Dynasty (秦朝), founded in 221 B.C, to the last dynasty, the Qing (清朝), which ended in A.D. 1911, each dynasty's characteristics evolved over time. Even so, what we see today, sometimes seems to be a repetition of what we have seen before.

> ### VIP Treatment
>
> In ancient days, when common people saw government officials passing along a street, they all huddled at the sides for the officials to pass through. The guards struck gongs and warned people to make way. This was called to step aside (回避). Today, something like that still goes on. Police traffic escorts sound sirens to clear the streets for very important government officials.

Traditions and Beliefs

Traditional practices and beliefs have evolved during different eras and dynasties. For example, it was believed that 5,000 years ago, during the Yangshao Culture (仰韶文化) period, people lived a stable life when agriculture and textiles were developed. They raised silkworms and began to weave silk clothing. As social classes developed, clothing became a sign of social status. During the Western Zhou Dynasty (1066–771 B.C.) every social class had its own style of clothing. From the Zhou Dynasty until the elimination of feudal society, emperors, empresses, imperial concubines, princes, princesses, officials, and common people were all attired in different ways.

Different Ethnic Groups

China has a total of 56 officially registered ethnic groups, of which 55 are minority ethnic groups, with one majority ethnic group (Han, 汉族). Although they make up only a small proportion of the overall Chinese population, the 55 minority ethnic groups are distributed widely throughout different regions of China. The regions where they are most concentrated are the Southwest, Northwest, and Northeast. Inner Mongolia, Xinjiang, Ningxia, Guangxi, Tibet, Yunnan, Guizhou, Qinghai or Sichuan, Gansu, Hubei, Hunan, and other provinces, all of which have substantial populations of ethnic minorities. Given such a diverse range of ethnic groups, it is understandable that beliefs and practices will vary.

Battle of the Sexes

At lunch with an American business associate, we happened to be talking about men from Shanghai. They have a reputation for being very good at housework. This was quite a surprise, since most Westerners believe that China is a largely male-dominated society. We then mentioned the "women's kingdom"(女儿国), a minority ethnic group in northwest Yunnan Province, where women can have several husbands. Most Westerners could not believe that such a place still exists in China.

Geography

Covering a total of 3,599,994 square miles of land, and 104,432 square miles of water, China is the fourth-largest country in the world, after Russia, Canada, and the United States of America. Climate and terrain vary widely. From a tropical climate in Hainan Island (海南岛) to the subarctic climate in Harbin (哈尔滨), these vast differences are reflected in a wide diversity of behavior and thinking.

Chinese People and the Unification of China

Diverse as they may seem, the Chinese people are actually quite unified. The most aggressive form of unification was a demonstrated by Emperor Qin Shi Huang (秦始皇) (221–210 B.C.). He introduced a common writing system, and over many centuries of evolution, the system has been refined to today's *Putonghua* (普通话) or Mandarin. Can you imagine the sheer synergy when 1.3 billion people can understand the same language! Although there is a single common language, each ethnic or dialect group still retains its dialect: for instance, Minnan (闽南) is spoken by people from Xiamen (厦门) and by people living south of the Minnan River (闽南河). Similarly, people from Shanghai speak their own dialect; people from Guangdong(广东) people speak Cantonese, Teochew, or other Guangdong dialects.

Speaking in Different Tongues

I know an American who was once a U.S. senior government officer. He was later assigned to Shanghai as the Senior Trade Representative of a city government in the United States. He is especially good at connecting with Chinese business people. His language capabilities include English, Chinese, Minnan, Cantonese, Berlayer (Indonesian Malay), French, and German. When I first met him, we actually communicated in Minnan (闽南). We felt very "comfortable" (亲切) with one another.

Language Gap

In 2002, when I first started my business, and made a trip to Shandong, I could not understand a single word of the Shandong dialect. Although the people could speak *Putonghua* (普通话) or Mandarin, it seemed that they did not wish to do so. We believe that they purposely wanted to speak in the dialect so that we could not understand them. We later had the officials who arranged the trip translate for us.

A Harmonious Society

The last 30 years of economic growth and reform have created substantial disparities in the distribution of wealth. People in the coastal cities have become much more prosperous than those in the inland areas. In an effort to address this situation, the Chinese government has introduced a series of policies, including ones to secure the equality and unity of ethnic groups, to give regional autonomy to ethnic minorities, and to promote respect for the faiths and customs of ethnic groups. These are to ensure that the different minority and majority groups live together in harmony (和谐). The policy of regional autonomy for ethnic minorities is the most fundamental. Under this policy, five autonomous regions—Inner Mongolia, Xinjiang, Guangxi, Ningxia, and Tibet, as well as numerous autonomous prefectures, counties, nationality townships, and towns—have been given a great deal of autonomy. With guidance from the Chinese government, ethnic minorities in areas that have been given regional autono-my are able to deal with their own affairs with a good deal of independence. Together with the Han people, the Chinese ethnic minorities have made great strides in building a prosperous and unified China. There is almost nothing that China would not do to guarantee stability (稳定) in the nation.

Throughout Chinese history, whenever the people have been dis-united, the Chinese have been bullied by foreigners. Unity is strength. It is commonly said that if a Chinese fights a Japanese, the Chinese will win. But if a group of Chinese fights a group of Japanese, the Chinese will lose. The Chinese firmly believe that they should not let foreigners sow seeds of disunity among them.

During the Qing Dynasty, the government was weak. Under pressure, it surrendered Hong Kong to the British. The Qing also allowed the Japanese to take over Taiwan. Those lessons have taught the Chinese well. They will not allow themselves to be humiliated again. China is now a force to be reckoned with.

Cultural Revolution and the Opening Up

The Cultural Revolution (1966–1976) had an enormous impact on the Chinese people. Scientists and intellectuals were made to work in farms. America and capitalism were considered to be China's enemies. Groups who were called the "intellectual youth" (知识青年 or 知青), such as young people born in Shanghai, were made to go to remote places such as Heilongjiang in the North. For a generation, people had to raise their children far from their original homes. Some, however, eventually returned home with their children.

For this reason, it is common to meet younger people whose par-ents come from different parts of China, which may turn out to be a vital piece of personal information. In a city such as Shanghai, business peo-ple are likely to meet people who hail from different parts of the country. By knocking down economic barriers over the last 30 years, China has taken its people from one extreme of social life to another. China's new social system is known as socialism with Chinese characteristics (中国特色社会主义).

The Need to Define Culture

It is very important to be aware of all these cultural issues when doing business in China.

Drinking Prowess

During a visit to Shandong, I was invited to dinner by my host company. There were several tables, and we were all seated in groups of 10. I had heard a great deal about the drinking prowess of the Shandong Chinese, but this was the first time I would get to fathom what it really meant.

Whenever you make a toast, you have to toast everyone at your table. (Meaning that for a table of 10, I had to toast 10 times.) My host told me that I should toast everyone twice in the first round because two is a good number (好事成双). Then after toasting twice, I was told that I had to go on and toast everyone four times for good wishes (四季发财). Then from four toasts, I went to six, then eight, then 10, and then 12, all for the sake of good wishes. (六六大顺, 八喜临门,十全十美, 十二月月好 respectively.) As you can imagine, different countries have different cultures, and drinking is an important part of the Chinese business culture.

The Different Generations

Today, we tend to identify three main groups of Chinese. The first consists of those from before 1949, also known as the old guard from their experiences of World War II. They have been through tremendous hardships, and are now very elderly. Their perception of the world is very different from the way younger people see the world. They pass on what they have learned to the young. They have been through the Cultural Revolution and experienced severe hardships. Hence, they treasure whatever they have been able to acquire. Next, are those born in or after the late 1970s. These people demonstrate strong aspirations and patience in their work. Traditions and history play a very important part in their lives. The last group is those born in the 1980s. They, unlike their grandparents, have not suffered hardships. They may believe that it is only natural to possess the things they have. In addition, this generation was born under the one-child policy. They are dearly cherished by their parents, and more exposed to Western cultures. Even before an interview, human resources managers can begin to under-stand interviewees by first focusing on the appropriate age group.

Chinese Education

Chinese education plays a huge role in molding character and attitudes. Thousands of years of Confucius' teachings are subtly embedded throughout the curriculum. As the saying goes, the impact of Chinese education is deeply rooted in the Chinese (根深地固).

Chinese literature ranges from *The Romance of the Three Kingdoms* (三国演义), *The Journey to the West* (西游记) to the deeply philosophical teachings of Sun Tzu (孙子) and Confucius (孔子).

Implications for Negotiating with the Chinese

The influence of the Chinese education system is widely reflected in the business world. When the Chinese negotiate, they tend to look at matters in depth, and over the longer term. They see a business relationship as one that occurs over a period of time, not as a point in time. The Chinese always have these principles at the back of their minds. This means that one has to be cautious when negotiating with the Chinese.

Aspects of Culture

Many newcomers to China will warm up to Chinese culture. It is important to gain a foothold in understanding these practices. Dining and entertaining provide good examples of Chinese attitudes.

Dining and Entertainment

Seating Arrangements

The host will want to be in the most dominant position during a meal, and will choose a seat that can signify his or her power. For instance, sitting with the back to the wall signifies a position of power (see Figure 16.1).

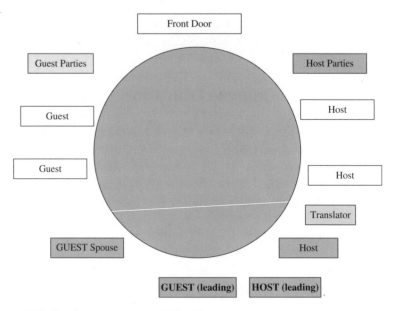

Figure 16.1 Seating Arrangements When Entertaining

Toasting

The Chinese love to toast their guests over a meal. When a host offers a toast, it is very rude not to accept. It is common for hosts to offer their guests many toasts over the course of a meal. Very often, toasting and drinking are ways to show appreciation to the host.

Types of Restaurant

The type of restaurant to entertain your guest is also of great significance. The elegance of the restaurants shows how much the host values the guest.

Drinking Tea

When the host pours tea into a cup, the guest makes a "Nod-and-Bow" gesture. This involves holding the index and middle finger together, bending them at the mid-joints, and knocking them slightly on the table, which symbolizes a nodding and bowing action. This practice came about during the reign of the Emperor Qian Long, as a mark of respect for the emperor.

Nod-and-Bow

During one of his many inspection trips across the country, disguised as an ordinary person, Emperor Qian Long first started the "Nod-and-Bow" practice. When drinking tea in a teahouse, the emperor poured tea for one of his subordinates. The subordinate was so flattered that he wanted to bow to the Emperor to express his thanks; however, such an action would have revealed the emperor's identity. The subordinate came up with an idea in a flash. He held his index and middle finger together, bending them at the mid-joints, and knocked them slightly on the table. Thus, he managed to symbolize the action of nodding and bowing, as was usually done in the emperor's palace, and expressed his thanks and respect for the emperor very tactfully. The "Nod-and-Bow" action later spread widely across the country, and is a commonly observed formality in many provinces.

Business Deals over Meals

In the Western world, business deals are usually negotiated and concluded in meetings, but in China, they are normally discussed and concluded over meals. So, it is very important to observe these details of hospitality that play such a huge role in the Chinese business world.

Gifts

Giving gifts was highly integrated into the Chinese traditional culture centuries ago, and has evolved to meet the needs of business practices. It is important to understand the reasons for giving gifts. It is a way of showing one's good will and warmth.

Gift giving has come a long way, and has gone through many changes. In the past, gifts came in many forms. Gold, silver, and money were very often used as gifts. However, in the modern era, people have begun to look upon gifts such as gold, silver, and money as bribery.

Gift giving in China requires an understanding of Chinese culture and history. Gifts are highly dependent on the occasion and traditions. For example, during the Mid-Autumn Festival, mooncakes are naturally used as gifts. People in the South may appreciate receiving gifts of smaller items, while people in the North enjoy receiving gifts that are larger in size.

Conclusion

Understanding the culture is very important when doing business in China. The country is diverse ethnically, and its extensive geography, its age-old historical background, and its kaleidoscope of beliefs, which vary across the land, make understanding Chinese culture quite difficult.

Difficult as it may be, understanding the Chinese culture is essential. It gives insight into the difficulties of doing business in China, making it easier to overcome them. To put it simply, a business deal can be won or lost, depending on how one performs over dinner.

17

Closing a Business in China

Every investor who enters China hopes to grow his business and do well. However, several reasons may lead to the eventual closing of the business, not all of them bad.

Manifold Reasons for Closing a Business

There are multiple reasons why an investor might want to cease a business in China. Here are some of the most common:

- The company may want to intensify its China operations, and therefore use a more versatile business vehicle, such as operating a Wholly Foreign-Owned Enterprise (WFOE). Usually, the investor will liquidate or close a representative office (RO) and set up a WFOE.
- Some investors choose to make a fresh start if the business license has expired.
- The company may decide to terminate its business operations in China because of poor performance.
- The latest regulations issued have opened the doors to industries that had previously been restricted. The company might want to expand its business via more independent and controlled legal

entities, such as the WFOE, or the Foreign Invested Commercial Enterprise (FICE).

• The current subsidiary structure no longer suits the needs of the foreign investor, and must be altered according to a different strategy, such as a merger and acquisition. In many mergers and acquisitions by a foreign investor in China, the original "shell" company is deregistered after absorbing an acquired entity.

Closing a business is like checking with the authorities, and having them inspect to make sure that all the bills have been paid. In real life, the process is almost never this easy. The inexperienced will most likely find the procedures of deregistering or liquidating an entity troublesome, and full of potential pitfalls. This is true even for deregistering an RO. That is why professional service experts offer full support in this area.

Closing the Business: Is There Another, Easy Way Out?

How does a company handle the procedures of closing down? Some investors may choose to just walk away. They may question the necessity of going through such a lengthy and bureaucratic deregistration process. The option of simply letting the subsidiary's license expire seems attractive and saves time, cost, and paperwork. However, if you fail to close your subsidiary entity properly and on time (30 days before its license expires), you may have to pay a fine and penalty. More threatening for foreign investors is the probability of being blacklisted. There is also the risk of penalties on the foreign investors, the WFOE's legal representative, or the RO's chief representative. This kind of record can seriously jeopardize all future business activities of the foreign investor in China. Therefore, the legal and proper way is a complete deregistration. With professional experts' support, the time and effort invested can be kept to a minimum.

Closing Down an RO

RO Upgrade to a WFOE or JV?

If you wish to sell, or import and export, receive RMB payments via local bank account, issue invoices to your local clients, or hire the staff directly instead of through a third-party intermediary agency, you will need to set up a WFOE or JV. You will also need to consider whether to keep the RO going, or to close and replace it with a local branch of the WFOE or JV.

You cannot just alter or upgrade the RO to a WFOE or a JV directly. This is a common misunderstanding. If the RO does not suit your needs anymore, just close it. You can deregister the RO at the same time that you establish the new WFOE or JV. However, if you wish to transfer your employees to the new WFOE or JV so as to maintain business continuity, foreign investors need to be precise in controling the schedule of both processes. The employee transfer can be made only after the business license of new WFOE or JV has been issued. Furthermore, the chief representative of the RO cannot be transferred to the WFOE or JV, unless the RO has been completely deregistered.

Situations That Render the RO Ineffective

Here are a few instances of situations in which an RO may not suit an investor's requirements any longer:

- The parent company has closed down, or changed business activities, so it may want to wind down the RO activities.
- The investor needs to upgrade its China subsidiary structure.
- The RO has not been operating in compliance with its business scope or the local regulations, and the foreign investor may wish to restart on a clean sheet.
- Expansion or cost saving requires relocation, making it necessary to close the old RO office, and register a new office.
- The investor needs its company to be able to conduct business: that is, enter into business contracts with suppliers directly, issue RMB billing and invoices, and collect local RMB revenue.

RO Liquidation Audit Report

When investors decide to close down the RO in China, they or their professional consultants should organize the liquidation audit report, which has to be submitted to the Tax Bureau as one of application documents. This RO liquidation audit report will focus on the individual income taxes of all RO employees, as well as the RO's corporate tax compliance. After all tax duties have been cleared, the related certificates and application documents, including the RO deregistration resolution by the parent company, have to be submitted to the tax authorities for approval. As long as the RO has no overdue taxes or other issues to be reported to the tax authorities, the deregistration procedures can begin.

Tax Clearance

First of all, applications need to be made at the Tax Bureau with related papers and the RO deregistration resolution of the parent company. In most situations, the required documents include an audit report up to the current month, RO tax returns, ledgers and vouchers, and tax registration certificates. If the RO is not subject to taxation, a notice from the Tax Bureau confirming this tax exemption status has to be presented.

Customs Clearance

Subsequently, the RO will need to obtain an Approval Certificate from the Customs Authority, together with a declaration of the reasons for the decision to close down operations in China. The same written explanations have to be given to all other bureaus involved in the closing procedures. In order to arrive at this stage, all outstanding customs duties have to be cleared, and the required documents have to be submitted.

Closing Bank Accounts

During the closing of a bank account, the check book, bank seals, and other related documents will be cancelled and returned to the bank. After the closure of the bank account, it is possible to withdraw or repatriate the remaining funds to the parent company.

Deregistering the RO Registration Certificate

In the next step, the RO will need to deregister the RO Registration Certificate with the State Administration Bureau for Industry and

Commerce (SAIC). In order to do so, all the previous approval notices from the Customs Authority and Tax Bureau should be shown to the SAIC, together with a board resolution from the parent company.

Submission and Return of Other Certificates

In the final step, the RO has to be deregistered from the Organization Code Administration Bureau and the Statistics Bureau.

The whole procedure usually takes eight to 12 weeks, depending on how carefully tax payments have complied with the laws and regulations in the past. The actual situation may be more complex than this brief summary. This is especially so if the RO's taxes, prior to deregistration, have not been compliant.

Liquidating a WFOE

The processes for WFOE liquidation and dissolution normally take about six to 12 months to complete. This should be considered normal. In other "abnormal" situations, such as complex tax clearance and debt settlement matters, it could even drag on longer.

Legal Framework

There are two types of liquidation when an enterprise closes operations: one is "normal liquidation," and the other is bankruptcy. "Normal liquidation," or nonbankruptcy liquidation, always results from a decision by the parent company. In normal liquidation, the company has the capability to pay up the bad debts to creditors, clear the outstanding taxes, and settle the staff salary and compensations. In contrast, bankruptcy always occurs when the total amount of loan and debts is larger than the company's assets. Also, bankruptcy is always triggered by creditors' claim in the People's Court.

The basic legal framework for company liquidation in China was originally provided in the Company Law for non-bankruptcy liquidation of domestic limited liability companies and companies limited by shares. Effective July 9, 1996, the Measures for Liquidation of Foreign Investment Enterprise in PRC ("Liquidation Measures") originally formed the legal basis for the regulations of nonbankruptcy liquidation of FIEs.

On January 15, 2008, the State Council issued Decree 516 and abolished the original Liquidation Measures. Although they had been in effect for more than 10 years, the liquidation measure was found to be unclear, and often could not settle a company's actual issues. It was also not aligned with the changes of the market reforms. Decree 516 now stipulates that nonbankruptcy liquidations will adhere to the Company Law and the bankruptcy liquidation will apply adhere to the Bankruptcy Law.

For those liquidations resulting from bankruptcy, the Chinese government has enacted unified bankruptcy legislation and promulgated the Enterprise Bankruptcy Law, effective June 1, 2007. According to Chinese regulations, enterprises that are qualified as legal persons include almost all types of enterprises, including private enterprises, state-owned enterprises, and foreign investment enterprises. Prior to the Bankruptcy Law, there were no special unified bankruptcy regulations in China. From now on, both domestic companies and foreign investment companies will adhere to the unified bankruptcy regulations.

For the first time, the Enterprise Bankruptcy Law covers commercial banks, insurance companies, and other financial institutions, including securities companies. Under the Bankruptcy Law, applications for the bankruptcy of such entities can only be made by their supervisory and regulatory bodies, which are under the State Council. The Bankruptcy Law also stipulates that the State Council may formulate implementation procedures for bankruptcy of financial institutions, in accordance with the Bankruptcy Law, and other relevant laws and regulations.

However, the Enterprise Bankruptcy Law is not applicable to partnerships and sole proprietorships. These areas are not covered in Chinese laws and regulations.

Bankruptcy Liquidation

Under the Bankruptcy Law, debtors can apply for liquidation, restructuring, or conciliation based on the following situations:

- Failure to clear debts as due
- Insufficient assets to repay all debts
- Obvious incapability to pay up debts
- Likelihood of inability to repay debt

The Bankruptcy Law combines international standards with the needs of modern Chinese society. For example, it establishes a new order for the discharge of creditors' interest, which complies better with international conventions, and better protects investors' and lenders' interests.

Companies filing for bankruptcy after the promulgation of the law will be required to first pay creditors with secured property, and then pay wages, medical, insurance, and other compensation they owe to their employees. Traditionally, compensation and insurance for employees had been paid first, and sometimes even secured property, including collateral to banks, had been used to finance the payment.

With regard to salaries and social insurance that are owed, if these have been incurred prior to June 1, 2007, the staff should take part in the proceeds of the assets distribution on a priority basis after insolvency costs and expenses have been covered. If the staff is compensated insufficiently, the balance of their claims should be repaid through realization of the secured assets prior to the secured creditors, who only thereafter enjoy the proceeds of their secured assets. But if wages or social security claims were incurred after June 1, 2007, the staff should only have a priority right against the secured creditors, with regard to the realization of unsecured assets of the debtor. Any proceeds of secured assets belong to the secured creditors on a priority basis.

After payment of liquidation expenses, salaries, social insurance and compensation for employees, taxes as well as settlement of liabilities, the remaining assets of the company should be distributed by the liquidation committee to the shareholders according to their equity or shareholding ratio.

Nonbankruptcy Liquidation

According to the Corporate Law, a WFOE may be dissolved if any of the following circumstances apply:

- The term of business operation as prescribed by the Articles of Association expires, or any of the matters for dissolution as prescribed in the Articles of Association of the company occurs.
- The shareholders' meeting or the shareholders' assembly decides to dissolve the business.

- It is necessary to dissolve due to a merger or a spinoff of the company.
- Its business license is canceled, or it is ordered to close down or to be dissolved according to law.
- Other reasons for dissolution stipulated in the original Articles of Association have occurred.
- The company runs into serious difficulty in its operations or management to cause the interests of the shareholders to suffer a heavy loss if it continues to exist, and these problems cannot be solved by any other means. The shareholders is granted the dissolution of the company by the People's Court.

Preapproval and Dissolution Commencement Date

During liquidation procedures, the dissolving company will need the preapproval of the original approving authority. After the shareholders and BOD have passed the liquidation resolution, the company should inform the authority of its intention to be dissolved. The original approval authority will review and judge whether the company is truly facing the matters giving cause to dissolution of the company. After preapproval, the authority will issue a notice so that the company can start the dissolution and liquidation procedures. The date of issue of such a notice will be the dissolution commencement date. This date is a key point during liquidation audits.

Establishing a Liquidation Committee

A liquidation committee should be formed within 15 days of the dissolution commencement date. This committee is appointed by the Board of Directors. The liquidation committee will take charge of all the liquidation work, and settle the company's assets. The liquidation committee should consist of at least three members appointed by the Board of Directors. The legal representative of the company should be a compulsory member of the liquidation committee. The other person may come from the directors, finance manager, debtors' representatives, and certified public accountants from a CPA firm and lawyers from a law firm.

The liquidation group will exercise the following functions during the process of liquidation:

1. Terminating the employment contracts, and settling compensation for employees.
2. Liquidating the properties of the company, producing balance sheets, and asset checklists.
3. Making a written notice to known creditors, and making a public announcement to notify unknown creditors.
4. Handling and liquidating the business of the company that has not been completed.
5. Evaluating, or outsourcing a qualified public accountant to evaluate, the appraisal and valuation of assets (this acts as the basis for calculation and distribution of assets).
6. Clearing off the outstanding taxes, and the taxes incurred in the process of liquidation.
7. Clearing off all the company's claims, credits, and debts.
8. Disposing of the residual properties after the company's debts have been paid.
9. Representing the company in civil proceedings in which the company may be involved.
10. After settlement of all the debts, generating a liquidation report, and submitting it to the Board of Directors and shareholders meeting for their approval.

Public Announcement of Liquidation

The liquidation committee should, within 10 days of its formation, notify the known creditors, and make a public announcement within 60 days in specified newspapers. Creditors should, within 30 days of receipt of a notice, or within 45 days of the issuance of the public announcement, declare amounts owing by the company to the liquidation committee.

To declare outstanding debts, a creditor should describe relevant matters, and provide relevant evidentiary materials. The liquidation group should record the debts declared, and may not clear off the debt of any creditor during the period of debt declaration.

Tax Clearance

In the case of disbanding, bankruptcy, business suspension and restoration, or other processes that result in termination of tax payment obligation, the company should bring the relevant documents and materials to the Tax Bureau of the original registration for tax deregistration, before the deregistration of the business license from the SAIC. Companies that do not need to deregister with the SAIC or other department, according to rules, should go to the original tax department of registration for deregistration within 15 days, after the date of approval or announcement of termination by the relevant department.

Companies that need to change the tax department of registration due to changes of business location should bring the relevant documents and materials to the tax department of registration for deregistration, before making registration changes with the SAIC within 30 days after the date of deregistration of tax.

WFOE Liquidation Audits

The liquidation audit report is a very important document during the liquidation procedures. According to the different local authorities' requirements, the liquidation audits may sometimes be required twice in the process:

1. *Preliquidation Audit Report.* This is provided when the dissolution and liquidation application is submitted to the authorities and the preapproval by the original authorities. This report focuses on the financial performance of the company from incorporation to the liquidation commencement date, especially for the six months before the liquidation commencement date. Hence, this report will act as the basis of calculation and distribution of liquidated proceeds.

2. *Liquidation Audit Report.* This report will be issued when all the deregistration procedures have been completed. The liquidation audit will focus on the completeness and truth of information about assets, the distribution of liquidated proceeds, and the liquidation expenses during the liquidation period. The liquidation audit report, as the proof of the completeness of the liquidation, will be kept by the investors together with accounting books and commercial contracts for at least 10 years.

Generally, the liquidation audits will clarify issues relating to:

1. The financial performance of the company for the six months before the liquidation commerce date
2. The completeness and truth of information on assets, such as
   - Whether fixed assets are legally owned by the company
   - Whether intellectual properties are legally owned by the company
   - Whether the registered capital has been fully injected by the investor, and verified by a CPA firm
   - Whether the properties assessment and appraisal by the company is reasonable
   - Whether the calculation of accounts receivable is correct
   - Whether the bad debt write-off are properly authorized
   - Whether the debts and loans of company are properly settled
   - Whether the bank account records are complete
   - Whether disposal of fixed assets is approved by the Tax Bureau
   - Whether investment assets are recorded and distributed correctly
3. The liabilities of the company, such as:
   - Whether the customs duty has been cleared successfully by the Customs Authority
   - Whether salaries, mandatory welfare, and other social contributions are calculated correctly
   - Whether taxes payable, including company income taxes, business taxes, withholding taxes, and individual income taxes, have been cleared properly
   - Whether other liabilities have been cleared properly
4. The liquidation expenses include expenses for management, expenses for public announcements, lawsuits and arbitration, consulting service fees for members of the liquidation committee, and other expenses that occurred during the liquidation. The audit is to check on whether these expenses were spent in compliance with the law.

Unused Raw Materials and Imported Equipment

A foreign invested manufacturing company should ensure that unused raw materials and imported equipment have been properly disposed of or dealt with. If a manufacturing enterprise has been enjoying exemptions from import customs duties and liquidation in advance that cannot meet the original operation period required by the Customs Authority, this enterprise should pay back the exempted importation customs duties, according to the proportion of actual operation period.

Deregistration of Other Certificates

Upon completion of the liquidation procedures, the liquidation committee should submit the liquidation report, certified by the Board of Directors and the Shareholders Meeting, to the original approval authority for approval. After that, the liquidation committee should return its business license, and deregister all the certificates issued by relevant governments. After deregistration, the company can repatriate the remaining funds back to the foreign investors.

Although some would view the liquidation as a tedious and boring process in China's bureaucratic environment, it is nevertheless very important for foreign investors to ensure that it is carried out properly when ending a business. Any other way out—even if it is the result of ignorance—will create more complex issues and potential pitfalls.

Index

201